Executing Your Business Transformation

Executing Your Business Transformation

How to Engage Sweeping Change Without Killing Yourself or Your Business

Mark I. Morgan

Andrew B. Cole

David R. Johnson

Robert J. Johnson

JOSSEY-BASS
A Wiley Imprint
www.josseybass.com

Published by Jossey-Bass
A Wiley Imprint
989 Market Street, San Francisco, CA 94103-1741—www.josseybass.com

Jossey-Bass books and products are available through most bookstores. To contact Jossey-Bass directly call our Customer Care Department within the U.S. at 800-956-7739, outside the U.S. at 317-572-3986, or fax 317-572-4002.

Jossey-Bass also publishes its books in a variety of electronic formats. Some content that appears in print may not be available in electronic books.

Library of Congress Cataloging-in-Publication Data
Executing your business transformation : how to engage sweeping change without killing yourself or your business / Mark I. Morgan . . . [et al.].
    p. cm.
Includes bibliographical references and index.
ISBN 978-0-470-47440-2 (cloth)
1. Organizational change. 2. Strategic planning. 3. Success in business. I. Morgan, Mark I.
HD58.8.E974 2010
658.4′06-dc22

2009047107

Printed in the United States of America
FIRST EDITION

HB Printing 10 9 8 7 6 5 4 3 2 1

Contents

Executing Your Business Transformation

INTRODUCTION

The Transformation Challenge

Jeff sat in the conference room after the management team reviewed the performance of the organization. As he projected forward three to five years to the results that the board of directors and analysts were expecting, one thing seemed obvious: the strengths of his organization today would not deliver the results of tomorrow. Every piece of evidence told him that he couldn't expect to grow the organization without selling more solutions along with products. Historically, selling products had been good enough for Jeff's company, but price pressure and market saturation eroded margins and decreased available market share. Jeff's team made reductions in costs to create a lean organization, but had run out of places to cut without hitting an artery. As a result, Jeff asked himself the question that all CEOs faced with obsolescence do: "How can I transform the organization from a seller of products to a provider of higher-value-added offerings or solutions?"

If you and your organization are facing a similar situation, you are not alone. "Jeff" is symbolic of hundreds of leaders contemplating the solution to the "solutions business," where maintaining the relationship with the customer demands offering a greater range of options than the simple product transactions that got you where you are today. This change seems an obvious extension of an existing business model. The logic of selling more to your existing customers is not new. Studies have shown how expensive acquiring entirely new customers can be. However, the plot thickens when we explore the difference between line extension and relationship change. For example, if we are a maker of dish soap and we add another household cleaner to the mix, that is not too big of a leap. But when we are a maker of dish soap and we want to add maid services to do the dishes, it becomes a little trickier. If this scenario sounds farfetched, consider the number of companies that are attempting to do this. Best Buy acquired Geek Squad in order to move from distributing products to providing products and services. Other big companies, such as IBM, Cisco, HP, Wipro, Monsanto, APC, Schneider Electric, and AVNET, have also undertaken their own version of the move from dish soap to maid services. Transforming a products company into a solutions company can be daunting, but does not have to be a mystery.

If you picked up this book, you are certainly in the midst of some sort of organizational change. At the time of this writing, the stock market has taken a huge setback, layoffs are in full swing, the U.S. government is making a transition of power, and global bailouts are at unprecedented levels. All comparisons to prior times are useless because we are in unexplored territory. The question to ask yourself is not whether your organization is engaged in change, but rather what side of the change curve you are on. Are you ahead of the curve, which means you have some time to get things together? Or are you behind the curve, where the phrase *burning platform* seems appropriate? There are no other options, because change is not an option—it is a requirement. It is also the most easily predicted of all phenomena; you are 100 percent guaranteed to always need to change. If you are not changing, you are becoming irrelevant. So your concern is not whether or not to change, but rather how and how much to change.

Given that all organizations struggle with change, it is interesting to note that all organizations seem to respond in one of two ways. First, there are companies that change only when a burning platform is evident. Consider how the airline industry responded after 9/11, suddenly implementing new cockpit doors on airplanes even though the idea was twenty years old. Second are organizations that are resistant to coaching. These organizations have leaders who "already know" and are resistant to learning anything new. Yogi Berra was fond of saying that "there are some people that, if they don't know, you can't tell them." In this book, we provide a set of lessons for both types of organizations. We hope to find teachable and coachable readers.

Turning Up the Flame on More Burners

Over the last two decades, there has been a greater drive among a broad range of businesses to accomplish what IBM accomplished in the 1990s: complete organizational transformation. When IBM added IBM Global Services to its brand, it engaged in a level of organizational transformation that had no contemporary equal. Today, the pursuit of organizational transformation to offer both products and solutions occurs in companies ranging from nuts-and-bolts providers to network software providers and everything in between. Whether you are SouthCo looking to create customer touch-point solutions, Wipro working to become a "trusted adviser," APC developing data center solutions, or Monsanto seeking to add more value to your customers by helping them maximize their crop yields, the story is the same. Companies are working toward higher-value transactions with higher operating margins that cannot be reached with products alone.

But what is driving this change? Two things: commoditization and saturation. Commoditization happens because most products compete on price, and as most cost-saving and supply-chain options for exploiting low-cost labor markets are available to almost all competitors, the inevitable result is that the profit is squeezed out of products at an increasing rate. To respond effectively to commoditization, an enterprise must provide something that is difficult for its competitors to replicate. Increasingly, this means offering a unique combination of products and services that focus on solutions to business problems as opposed to product features and benefits. Offering solutions with products is not a new idea; what is new is the speed at which this change must be implemented for companies to remain competitive.

The second driver is saturation. Saturation happens when a market segment can no longer absorb more product volume. Consider Starbucks's situation. Starbucks was expanding nonstop until companies such as Peet's, It's a Grind, and, most recently, McDonald's began to penetrate Starbucks's market share with a lower price point. McDonald's can now offer a similar product for far less and can use its savings to take share away from Starbucks. When many people are looking for every conceivable reduction in spending and there are numerous caffeine vendors to be found, Starbucks needs to change to survive; it must consider how to expand channels, change product lines, add fractal products to the coffee offer, or become a "beverage solution provider." In Starbucks's case, there really is no services option readily available to it. Food, music, and other fractal products that go with the coffee experience are about as close to solutions as the company is likely to get. It is conceivable that Starbucks could expand on its core competency in environmentally conscious supply chain management and create a new consultancy called Starbucks Global Services. In any case, the Starbucks lesson allows us to see that under certain market conditions and with the expansion of alternatives, growth becomes difficult without a significant shift in the organization.

Easier Said Than Done

Although it may be easy to decide to transform into a solutions organization, few have been successful. There is an old joke about five frogs who are sitting on a log, and four decide to jump off. However, all five frogs remain on the log after making the decision because deciding to do something is very different than actually doing it. This joke seems a very appropriate analogy to organizational transformation. In our experience, it takes most organizations two business cycles after declaring the jump from the log to realize that they do not know how to change the organization. Part of the delay seems to come from a lack of understanding as to the scope of the changes that are required in making transformation happen. The broad range of decisions required for transformation results in some decisions not being made because the organization does not recognize the need for a decision. We refer to this as the "fish don't know water" syndrome: many teams of executives simply do not see the organizational issues until they are taken out of the situation, like the fish that don't experience the water until they are out of it and into the boat. The other reason for the delay seems to be a result of making decisions in isolation. There are many interrelated decisions required in order to make transformation work. Isolated decision making that comes from siloed thinking can stop transformation dead in its tracks. To improve decision making, an organization must understand and successfully deal with three realities of transformation: core, context, and capability.

Transformation in a Nutshell

Why didn't railroad companies evolve into trucking and air freight? Why didn't the U.S. Post Office evolve into UPS, FedEx, DHL, and Airborne? Why didn't Microsoft evolve into Google, Yahoo, Netscape, Facebook, and YouTube?

Inertia.

The principle of inertia is that things at rest tend to stay at rest, and things in motion tend to stay in motion. Organizations have inertia. They tend to find a groove (say, products) and stay in that same groove. To get out of one groove (products) and get into another groove (solutions), an organization must address the three realities of all organizations. First is the organization's foundation, which we call the organizational **core**. Second is the organizational building blocks on top of the foundation, which we call organizational **context**. Third is the fundamental abilities of the organization, which we call organizational **capability**.

Legacy or Leg Irons? Dealing with Core

Organizational roots run deep. Businesses constructed around a strong formative idea that resonates with both staff and customers create strong, long-lasting roots of tradition and culture. These roots, which are critical to the success of the company in its growth stages, can become a liability when the company needs to change direction. The Fortune 500 of today contains a small percentage of the Fortune 500 of twenty years ago. For example, IBM came very close to extinction. Transformation was necessary to its survival, and as part of the process of transformation, a part of IBM's core needed to be replaced.

An organization's core is composed of its purpose, long-range intention, and identity. Purpose is the reason why the organization exists. Long-range intention is the mission of the organization or what the organization is dedicated to in the long run, such as a cure for diabetes. Identity is who the company is. Although some of these aspects may be informal, they are always present to some degree. During organizational transformation, there is often a conflict between what needs to happen for the company to transform, and its perception of its purpose, long-range intention, and identity. Until the organization deals with the necessary changes relative to its core, the transformation will likely suffer false starts and the effects of inertia. The most difficult aspect for many organizations is identity. If an organization has historically been an efficient producer of products, it may have a difficult time overcoming the perceptions held by customers and staff. Getting the market to see you as a solution provider when it has you categorized as a product producer is no small undertaking. A huge investment may be required to shift brand perception in the marketplace.

An organization can significantly reduce transformation time by carefully evaluating how transformation relates to the existing organizational core. A company that attempts transformation through acquisition, for example, often finds out that when two companies that have different core purposes combine, the only transformation that is taking place is one of acquisition capital into wasted effort. By understanding the impact of transformation at the core, leaders will make better decisions as to the set of investments to be made. The cost of merging operations in order to extract so-called synergies is just the start of the investment stream required for transformation. Here are the aspects of organizational core, considered in terms of transformation:

- *Purpose*. Is the organization fundamentally dedicated to discovery of new things, doing known things in an outstanding way, serving the masses, or saving the day in heroic fashion? As Nikos Mourkogiannis pointed out in his book *Purpose* (Palgrave Macmillan, 2007), great companies are built on strong purpose. In transformation, you need to take into account what is kept, what is changed, and what is discarded with regard to purpose.

- *Identity*. If a company has been a maker of automotive mufflers for a century and leaders are now contemplating offering franchises in muffler repair as a vertical integration form of transformation, they should fasten their seat belts. As they find out that the market does not recognize them in this space and that their internal competencies do not include business management or financial and operations expertise, they will see their investment requirements explode. Many organizations discount the cost of moving away from their core identity and the strengths of their organizational DNA.

- *Long-range intention*. At the farthest point on the horizon, what is the organization dedicated to? This is a hard question for organizations to come to grips with and an even more difficult one in times where mere economic survival looms large. Nevertheless, answering this question is critical. A lack of long-range vision is chronic in organizations. So much focus goes to quarterly and year-over-year metrics that long-term thinking is almost a lost art. If the best way to predict a future is to create it, then we need to name what that future holds.

"We Don't Have Time for a Blueprint! Let's Just Start Building": Dealing with Context

In California there is a tourist attraction called the Winchester Mystery House. Turns out that there is not a lot of mystery, but there *is* a lot of house. Sarah Winchester, believing herself cursed by Native Americans who had been killed by Winchester firearms, dedicated a large amount of her life and money to launching a never-ending stream of building projects for the purposes of staving off the curse and prolonging her life. Whether real or imagined, her core belief that she was cursed drove the project investments she made and the structure she created. The house, with its stairways that lead nowhere and doors that open into thin air, reflects Sarah's unstable mind or "core." Core drives context. Some organizations fail in their attempts at transformation because they haven't considered how their core and context must change for the organization to transform. When core and context are out of alignment, project investments are likely to lack coherence.

To get a rough idea of how complicated it can be to transform an organization's context, consider that all of the following aspects that create context must be orchestrated in a synchronized fashion to create organizational transformation:

- *Goals*. The goals of the transformed organization are often not the goals of the past or present. For example, if an organization is working on becoming a global services provider, goals that are formulated around local performance at the expense of global performance derail transformation. The odd thing about goals is that nobody can tell anybody else what they should be. In the same way that purpose, identity, and long-range intention are chosen, so too are goals. Perhaps because goals are a matter of choice and not of requirement, organizations tend to adopt a default set of goals based on standard economic factors. Without a declaration of goals, transformation is fatally wounded before it is even begun. After all, without goals, all an organization can do is shoot first and then call whatever it hits, the target. Conversely, when a company articulates its goals, leaders can begin to design the path forward and marshal the resources toward achieving them.

- *Metrics*. What is the driving factor? Is it regional profit, customer share of wallet, global sales, global margin, account growth, percentage of revenue generated by global accounts, service revenue, product revenue, professional service margins, professional service utilization ... or something else? People respond to what generates results for them. Transformation requires a new metric set. Designing and implementing new metrics require investment in metric design, systems, and processes.

- *Central strategy*. Has the organization historically been a cost leader? A solutions strategy requires the organization to create differentiation that goes beyond cost leadership. Strategy is the path that is taken to achieve goals. The ability to change paths and operate on a new path requires new competencies, which come from focused development and investment. The embedded mentality of cost leadership may not suit differentiation very well. A focus on total efficiency may interfere with what the organization needs moving forward. Over time, an organization takes on an unconscious competence relative to its central strategy. When transformation requires that the central strategy change, the organization will not change without a sustained investment in molding new competencies. One of the ways this shift is accomplished is through modification of internal and external branding, which also entails a significant investment.

- *Culture*. What is the balance between control, collaboration, cultivation, and competence? And is there passive, aggressive, or constructive organizational behavior? The ability of an organization to adapt may well rest with its ability to address culture simultaneously with performance. What often gets missed in transformation efforts is that an organization's culture undergoes change as a result of new goals based on new metrics, structure, and strategy, and changes to the organization's core. Attempting to change culture as a stand-alone initiative without considering the organization's new goals, structure, strategy, purpose, identity, and long-range intention not only wastes time but also sets the organization back.

- *Structure*. Structure is largely a tool to be used when designing transformation and becomes critical when considered along with goals and metrics, culture and strategy. For example, product companies tend to become siloed by function where the company's strength and power reside in the functional organizations. In the solutions business, cross-functional work becomes a necessity. Without a revision and redesign of the power structure, transformation is likely to get derailed. By focusing the organization on the productive use of the matrix structure, transformation can get on track.

- *Systems*. In a products organization, all the systems—information, hiring, communications, recognition, performance management, portfolio management—evolve to suit a products model. When an organization transforms, all the systems have to transform with it. This is not a small investment and is one of the highest-risk areas for transformation failure.

- *Markets*. When a company moves from products to solutions, there is often the perception that the company is going to sell a solution to its product customers. The problem with this scenario is that the person purchasing the product is usually in a different part of the organization than the purchaser of solutions. The contacts, the relationship, the pace of the sale, and the sales cycle are all different. Investment is needed under transformation to modify or create new go-to-market strategies, people skills, capabilities competencies, and systems.

- *Point of differentiation*. The whole point of transformation is to secure a new strategic position that is of higher value. What may change in the process is what gets optimized for the customer. In the past it may have been purchase price or delivery speed; now the organization must be designed around total cost of ownership, which takes into account the costs over the life of the product, not just the initial cost. Product companies tend to think "product out." "If you build it, they will come (to buy it)" is the assumption. Solution companies are "solution in" thinkers. The focus shifts from features and benefits to optimizing customer outcome, from sales as an event to sales as a system of value-added options, and from "designing a product to offer" to "offering to design a solution."

After considering all these aspects of organizational context, the organization must then examine what its capabilities are today and compare them to the capabilities needed in the future.

Ready, Willing, and Able: Dealing with Organizational Capability

For most organizations undergoing business transformation, the marketplace and customers have forced the issue. The question is not about readiness but about obsolescence. People who aren't willing to change need to find another bus. For the remainder, capability is the key. And developing capability is not free.

For an organization starting from scratch, such as Google, eBay, and Mozilla, the human resources side of the business is more straightforward than in situations where a company has thousands of people who are habituated into processes that must change in order to transform. Starting with a clean slate, the hiring processes can be tailored to attract the right skills, and the business processes can evolve with the business. Companies that have been around for years if not decades do not have this luxury. What is surprising to us is how early in the life of a company the patterns of behavior form. We have seen the creation of ruts in companies that are pre-IPO.

With an existing enterprise, in contrast, the inertia of the past becomes the baggage of the future. A company adopting a transformational strategy faces what we call *in-flight kite repair*. Businesses, unlike a kite, cannot be brought down to earth to work on and then relaunched into flight. Transformation is accomplished on top of full agendas. So the transformation must be done in-flight. This puts enormous pressure on four aspects of capability: portfolio management, program management, project management, and process management.

- *Portfolio management.* The way a company decides how to allocate scarce resources is central to transformation because there are multiple areas of investment that must be simultaneously reconciled in order to keep the kite flying. The first area comprises activities related to *working in the business,* which are those that are associated with today's revenue. Activities related to *working on the business* are those that modify existing processes and systems to improve the operation that exists today. The third area, *working to transform the business,* are those activities that modify the market offering, delivery processes, systems, structures, skills, competencies, and so on. Working to transform the business can get lost quite easily because the incremental investment to make it happen gets diluted or eclipsed by working in and working on the business.

- *Program management.* Transformation requires the integration of a large number of efforts into a coordinated set of activities. To manage the risk at critical interfaces, program management requires being able to identify the interdependency between projects that span across functions. This is an advanced skill that goes far beyond skill in project management. The requirement is to master the ability to maintain program unity while delivering complex and mission-critical initiatives.

- *Project management.* Transformation is ultimately delivered in work packages known as projects. Projects have a specific deliverable with a specific timeline and specific resources. The risk of transformation failure is inversely proportional to the ability to manage the projects that deliver it. There is a big difference between talking about change versus bringing it about. *Projects bring it about.*

- *Process management.* Many of the processes used today must be modified to support the transformed enterprise. An organization must be able to articulate the current process clearly enough to be able to identify required process changes. If an organization does not have process control as a mature competency today, the risk in transformation is that processes will be modified in ways that are either ineffective or damaging to the transformation effort.

Eye on the ball, shoulder to the wheel, ear to the ground, nose to the grindstone ... how can we work in that position?

Let's recap. What we're suggesting here is that transformation be executed in consideration of the purpose, long-range intention, and identity of the organization; it entails modification to goals, metrics, central strategy, culture, structure, systems, target market, and point of differentiation; it requires the critical capabilities of process management, project management, and program management, all under the comprehensive capability of portfolio management. You may be thinking that the kitchen sink is likely to get tossed into this discussion sometime soon. Tossing in the kitchen sink might in fact be necessary at some point in the journey toward transformation. The reality is that organizations have a tendency to enter transformation with more enthusiasm than comprehension. As a result, many struggle as they spin their wheels and become frustrated with the lack of progress.

The Eleven Lessons

What follows in this book is a set of lessons gained while working in and with organizations in the process of transformation. Our message is not prescriptive. Rather, our message is that there are specific, learnable aspects to transformation that any organization can apply. The lessons are not written in any particular order, nor are they meant to be read all at once. Some of them deal with core aspects, some with context, some with capability. The final chapter looks at the path forward in organizational transformation, where the lessons are yet to be learned. Following is a summary of what you can expect to find between the covers of this book.

Once upon a Time in Transformation—Chapter One briefly describes the companies that inspired the lessons in the book. All the companies illustrated are successful organizations that in one way or another serve as great examples of creating changes proactively.

Lesson 1 (What got you here may kill you there)—Chapter Two examines the tendency of organizations to hang on to legacy ways of doing business when the business results still look good, only to find out that they are behind the curve in terms of generating needed change.

Lesson 2 (Yesterday's leadership skills may prevent tomorrow's success)—Chapter Three delves into what happens when we find the enemy and it is us.

Lesson 3 (There is no strategy if nobody knows what to do)—Chapter Four offers insight into how smart-sounding, unintelligible presentations don't add up to effective action, and what to do about it.

Lesson 4 (Transforming strategy requires more than expensive software)—Chapter Five is dedicated to the objective of bridging the gap between strategic planning and portfolio management, whereby the decision system translates transformation into investment decisions.

Lesson 5 (Transform Human Resources into a strategic advantage)—Chapter Six brings to light the central role of HR in transformation and discusses why HR is the biggest missing piece in most transformation.

Lesson 6 (Your customers are always right, except when they aren't)—Chapter Seven deals with customer-facing issues. In transformation, the definition of the customer changes, and the role of customer feedback changes as the organization changes.

Lesson 7 (Don't let analysts run your business)—Chapter Eight deals with the expectations game. How do you get the street satisfied and the organization transformed—and keep your job? This chapter deals with how to make decisions without undue influence from those with no accountability.

Lesson 8 (*Merger* is not a four-letter word)—Chapter Nine provides an unconventional and powerful way to address mergers so as to prevent the typical loss of value experienced in most company marriages.

Lesson 9 (Who melted my cheese?)—Chapter Ten examines how the heat and pressure of mergers and acquisitions have an impact on transformation. Especially when they *are* the transformation. The impact on people is enormous, and this chapter deals with keeping human assets intact.

Lesson 10 (Spin is overrated for creating value)—Chapter Eleven examines the effect of complete and utter candor in the face of merger—where the spin is replaced with unvarnished truth.

Lesson 11 (Consultants are not an excuse for not knowing your business)—Chapter Twelve provides information on the use of consultants and how to get a sound "return on consulting."

Lessons, Not Best Practices

Few things cause an allergic reaction among us quite like someone throwing out the idea of adopting best practices. A best practice is what used to work for some other company in its context and in its time. Bleeding people to cure their illnesses was once a best practice. A six sigma bleeding practice will not negate the fact that the practice is flawed from the point of view of medical treatment efficacy. George Washington learned the hard way. He ultimately went into shock as a result of bleeding, while a leading practice called a tracheotomy was available but not attempted because his doctors refused to abandon best practice.

Innovation does not come from the adoption of best practice. It comes from looking upstream from best practices. Before something was a best practice, it was a leading practice. Before that it was an experiment, before that it was a theory, before that it was a thought, and before that it was an observation. What gave rise to the value of the observation was experience or wisdom or intelligence. What is contained in this book is wisdom gained through experience, given with the intention that you will form your own theories as to how it applies to your organization, set up some experiments, and develop some relevant leading practices that are best for your organization in its circumstances.

1

ONCE UPON A TIME
IN TRANSFORMATION
A Learning Opportunity

Much has been written about turnarounds at places like General Electric and IBM, where heroic, high-pressure, time-constrained transformation saved the dying business. What is missing from the literature is the less-publicized but still heroic stories of organizations that changed before they got to the brink of disaster. Although studying train wrecks can shed light on how train wrecks happen and how to clean them up, the value of such study is limited if you are seeking to make changes before disaster happens. In this case, the best set of lessons comes from organizations that changed before it was too late.

American Power Conversion, ALLDATA (a subsidiary of AutoZone), A123 Systems, and portions of Monsanto represent the full spectrum of pre-IPO to large, mature companies that have been proactive in creating transformation. Although all these companies are at different stages of transformation, they have a remarkably similar set of challenges.

In this chapter, we provide a brief profile of these companies and lay out the issues of transformation they face or have faced. In each case, the company has undergone change proactively, and each has faced the issues associated with being forced "out of the box." Table 1.1 illustrates how the level of integration of a company's offer combines with the level of customization of an offer and suggests where incremental change stops and where transformation becomes an imperative.

In Table 1.1, box A represents companies that offer a single product or service. Their next stage of development is to sell combinations of parts, represented by box B. Companies in

Table 1.1

	Level of Customization		
Level of Integration	*Standard*	*Modified Standard*	*Custom*
Full System (Computing system)			
Subsystem (Computer)			
Assembly of Parts (Motherboard)	C		
Group of Parts (Kit of components)	B		
Detail Parts (Components)	A		

box B, seeking new growth opportunities, are tempted to offer assemblies, which are companies in box C. Consider Intel as an example of a company that grew from box B to box C. It started out selling microprocessors, then grew to sell chip sets and eventually motherboards for computers.

Once companies grow beyond the confines of these three boxes—that is, once customization reaches the modified standard level or full customization—the business requires significant transformation. The same applies moving in the direction of subsystems and full systems. Organizations will find that many of the success factors that made them a high performer in box A will become limiting factors as they attempt to take the company outside the box. In other words, the core competency of the original product-focused company isn't the same competency needed for system-level thinking and consultative market approaches. Although transformation is sometimes difficult and problematic, it is necessary for companies that have run out of market to capture or that are facing commoditization of their products. American Power Conversion is one example of a company faced with this scenario.

American Power Conversion

American Power Conversion (APC) started the way that many companies do: a collection of brilliant technical minds began to explore how to convert a technology into a useful product. In

APC's case, Neil Rasmussen, Emmanuel Landsman, and Irving Lyons got together to develop solar power conversion products. When the market for solar power products failed to materialize the way they envisioned, they orchestrated their first transformation. Their company produced a set of technologies used to create products for protecting computing devices, such as the personal computer, from suffering data loss as a result of power loss. Their basic product is known as an uninterruptible power supply (UPS).

A small New England–based company, APC grew from making a limited number of power-related products to providing a wide range of power solutions ranging from mobile power to data centers. Its transformation was enabled by its ability both to deliver a broad range of high-volume standardized products and to bundle products into solutions for highly complex enterprise applications. Critical to its success was its creative use of supply-chain design, sourcing strategy, global manufacturing capability, and the management of channel conflict in an all-channels strategy.

By 2003, the time had come for APC to get out of the box. Growth in the organization required a shift from its being a products-based company to one focused on bundled solutions. APC wanted to be ambidextrous, able to deliver both discrete products and bundled solutions. This goal threatened the organization's DNA as a products company—its roots, goals, metrics, structure, culture, and brand. Initial attempts to define a strategy for achieving such ambidexterity left the organization in a two-year stalemate.

What affected APC—and other companies in its situation—is that transformation required the company to continue to function productively in its base business while simultaneously building capability in other areas. APC's challenge was to take a company of thousands of employees distributed across sixty-seven countries, with expertise in volume production, and transform it into a company that could maintain this business while also providing systems made up of power conditioning subsystems, cooling subsystems, and software. In addition, the company had to respond to the concerns raised by analysts, customers, and consultants, and successfully manage its subsequent acquisition. The opportunity for confusion to take over was growing, people's cheese was being melted, leadership skills were being tested, and the HR people had their hands full, just to name a few challenges. Three of us worked inside APC, and one of us worked as a consultant. Our firsthand experience of assisting APC through its transformation inspired many of the lessons in this book.

ALLDATA

ALLDATA is an independent business unit owned by AutoZone, one of the largest distributors of automobile parts in the United States. ALLDATA creates repair information for the use of service personnel when making repairs to automobiles. When you take your car into a service center, the technician can use the ALLDATA subscription service to look up the part content and repair action for your specific car. This in turn allows for better service by repair facilities as well as greater confidence in estimating the time and cost of the repair.

ALLDATA's core business is acquiring data, arranging them in searchable fashion, and selling subscriptions to the database. There is limited bundling required, and it is not a subsystem or system-level sale. Aside from the occasional modified standard or custom application, the company's business model is primarily that of a product line.

ALLDATA's advantage is the quality of its data. It provides data that are true to the original equipment manufacturer (OEM), and has also developed the same service for companies that do body and frame repairs. The company has been very successful in the automotive repair world, and owns a large percentage of the market. Its share is so strong, in fact, that there is limited access to greater share. In order to grow, ALLDATA will need ongoing transformation. It will either have to find new markets for its existing model or move into products and services that are closer to a subsystem or system-type sale.

Luckily, ALLDATA's offerings for shop management software and shop marketing applications can aid the company in its transformation. The shop management software allows businesses to integrate the repair order, work order, service record, and invoicing functions; the shop marketing applications can be used for client acquisition and retention. But even though shop management and marketing complement ALLDATA's central business of repair data offerings, the latter is sold and serviced very differently. It is a big step to move from supplying a standard product to every customer to offering a solution that is dependent on the specific customer. As is true for many companies there are changes required in every aspect of the organization: the core, context, capabilities, capacities, competencies, and customer outcome.

Monsanto

Suppose you have a tomato farm that has a 1 percent slope with a 23-degree south-by-southwest exposure at 14 degrees north latitude with semialkaline soil and water that contains a large amount of sulfur. Monsanto probably has a tomato seed for you. Or what if you have a weed problem, and you are seeking not more plants but fewer? Monsanto can also help you with that—its Round-Up™ is an iconic brand in the herbicide market.

Monsanto enjoys a level of differentiation from other plant seed and herbicide producers in that it has developed food seeds that are resistant to Round-Up. This allows entire crops to be sprayed, killing the weeds without affecting the crop. These seeds are such a unique differentiator for Monsanto that the company is currently suing DuPont for allegedly violating Monsanto's patents in this area. Without this advantage, Monsanto faces commoditization of its seeds and would need to find other sources of competitive advantage.

But Monsanto is ahead of the curve. The company has begun to create a system-level consultancy to help farmers maximize crop yields. It may sound simple to leap from selling seeds to helping farmers increase yield, but the business model required to make that happen is anything but simple. This is what makes Monsanto a prime example of transformation. The organization that is designed to optimize research and development for producing seeds is not the same organization that is designed to work collaboratively across business functions and agricultural systems and to develop a profit value chain based on services. Monsanto is about as far from APC, A123, and ALLDATA as can be, yet it faces the same questions about what to do about getting out of the box.

A123 Systems

A123 at the time of this writing is a pre-IPO company that has a phenomenally bright future in the business of producing products and systems based on a battery technology known as Nanophosphate™ lithium ion. A123 describes it this way:

> A123 Systems is now one of the world's leading suppliers of high-power lithium ion batteries using our patented Nanophosphate™ technology designed to deliver a new combination of power, safety and life.
>
> Our breakthrough technology, innovative multinational manufacturing model, team of tier-one investors, and experienced executives are providing the power to change the game for today's Transportation, Electric Grid Services and Portable Power manufacturers.
>
> For larger projects that require volume manufacturing, we operate state-of-the-art manufacturing facilities in Asia which have the capacity to scale to millions of battery packs per year, and we are currently expanding our manufacturing capacity in the U.S.

Origin of Our Name

A123 Systems owes its name to the Hamaker force constant which is used to calculate the attractive and repulsive forces between particles at nano dimensions, and which begins "A123 . . ."

The scope of applications for this technology ranges from power tools to automobiles to buses to power grid applications. Because of the vast array of opportunities for a company with disruptive technology such as A123, the company needs to decide whether or not to change its business model—and it hasn't even gone public yet. The lesson here is that transformation is an imperative not just for mature companies but for any company that faces the challenge of either moving on to something else or becoming irrelevant.

Summary

Business books are often written in an opportunistic way. At the time of this writing, there are countless books on how to cope with hard times, coinciding with current economic woes. Chances are, the titles would be different if the economy were in different shape. How convenient it is to jump on a bandwagon and ride as far as possible. This is not an opportunistic book. Nor is it the spinning of some business fable about a grand savior or a flaming defeat. The companies we refer to here are examples of transformation that provide valuable insight if viewed constructively and in their context. We intend none of the companies used here as illustration to be a subject of criticism or praise necessarily. They are all respected and respectable enterprises and, when taken collectively, represent examples of transformation that in our opinion form a valuable basis for learning. Although there are huge differences between the companies we discuss, there are similarities in the underpinning issues they face. That is the key to understanding transformation. Although businesses may differ in market, product, or service, they all share a set of common lessons that can be of use to many companies because of the universal nature of the problems organizations face in transforming themselves.

2

WHAT GOT YOU HERE MAY KILL YOU THERE

Nothing fails like success.

—*Gerald Nachman*

During its development as a products producer, CanCo was one of the few companies to find a way to master the go-to-market process using multiple channels with minimum channel conflict. In addition to developing systems to source product production cheaply and globally, CanCo also created sophisticated ways of determining optimum order quantities and the most efficient way to ship the finished products. This allowed it to serve large-volume direct customers, its distributors, and its internal sales organization. All this process and system development work, combined with CanCo's leading-edge technology, made the company a tough competitor in its market.

Unfortunately, after two decades as a successful products producer, CanCo's product was suffering from commoditization, so the company decided to move toward more integrated solutions. However, this proved difficult for CanCo, as its strength was in producing large, efficient volumes of products in a wide mix of models and features. Producing extremely small volumes tailored for integrated solutions was not its forte.

In keeping with customer demand to enter the "solution space" while responding to emerging opportunities, CanCo decided to enter into a deal with a longtime product customer to create custom solutions. The customer, Tellcomm, engaged CanCo to build a large installation with CanCo's products integrated with products from other producers. Tellcomm benefited from this arrangement because working through CanCo allowed for a single point of contact rather than multiple interfaces. Tellcomm liked the arrangement of having a single supplier with broad accountabilities because it created "one throat to choke." It was CanCo's job to handle coordination, communication, and all other interface issues for the Tellcomm project.

A number of problems began to surface as CanCo began to serve Tellcomm's multifaceted needs. First, CanCo's ordering systems were not designed for small-volume orders, so a large amount of manually generated orders needed to be placed and tracked outside the basic systems. CanCo also ended up paying more for these smaller orders, and so lost the advantage of ordering larger volumes at lower costs per unit. In addition, CanCo had no way to reserve inventory for a future use, so parts were often not available when they were needed. Parts found to be out of stock in the United States often had to be shipped at a premium to fill a need, or a small quantity had to be produced in a very short time, which resulted in additional costs.

CanCo also lacked the required project management processes; in fact, the ability to lay out project plans and manage in accordance with the plan was nonexistent. The company had no system for ordering and tracking multiple interrelated parts that could then be put together in a kit arrangement, and there was no activity-based costing system for the overall effort, so capturing revenue based on nonproduct cost became impossible. Essentially, the Tellcomm project ran on an ad hoc basis with the project manager simply coping with the complexity of the task at hand.

At the end of the day, the Tellcomm project was acceptable to Tellcomm but a mixed bag for CanCo. Although CanCo had not embarrassed itself as a partner, there was almost no evidence of CanCo deriving any profit from the relationship. Indications were that it was a negative profit producer, but nothing certain could be said in this regard due to the lack of cost accounting. And even if CanCo wanted to try such an arrangement again in the future, the company couldn't scale this type of project due to a lack of proposal processes, contracting processes and systems, cost accounting systems, professional services infrastructure, and project and program management expertise.

In sum, what got CanCo to the top of its game was the mixture of product innovation and supply chain efficiency, which delivered low product cost at high levels of product performance. But these same systems became impediments to transforming part of the company into professional services offerings. Systems that are designed to optimize production cost fail when asked to deliver system integration. The lesson: what got CanCo here killed them there.

Misery Loves Company

Kodak taught us that just because you can make the best film in the world does not mean that you will be able to make that technology stretch forever. The same thinking that went into making better and better film and film cameras became Kodak's albatross when digital cameras came along. Saying that the image quality of film is superior to that of digital evidently does not matter when the customer is looking for instant gratification.

Polaroid provided the ultimate lesson in one-trick-pony history. Once a leader in innovative immediate-image cameras, the company soon became an also-ran when it tried to extend its "1-Step" product line into digital cameras. That decision resulted in its post–Chapter 11 acquisition. What got it there died there. In 2009, Polaroid discontinued manufacturing film.

Krispy Kreme is another example of a company with a very successful business plan that suddenly wasn't (C. Reidy, "The Rise and Fall of Krispy Kreme in New England," *Boston Globe*, July 23, 2006). When consumer backlash against carbohydrates combined with the company's numerous business missteps, Krispy Kreme's skyrocketing business model was brought to a sudden halt. The franchise model that helped it expand had become a liability.

Causes

There are many examples of companies in which something that made them successful in one area resulted in disaster in another. But what is missing from these stories—and what we will outline next—are the causes of this phenomenon.

Cause 1: Lack of Systems Thinking

Under the old English system of manufacturing, no two parts of a machine or firearm could be made identically. The assembly line hadn't been invented yet, so there was no standardization. Firearms had to be created one at a time by a single worker. Only after the development of a process for producing standardized interchangeable parts was it possible to assemble units efficiently.

Although we've come a long way in manufacturing, this problem still exists today in the form of interface incompatibility between subsystems. As a company begins to integrate its products and those of others into a solution, it is likely to encounter compatibility problems between its products and those of its suppliers. In CanCo's case, the company was working with products that were not designed to work together. In order to develop larger turnkey solutions for customers, CanCo needed to design products with the system in mind. A focus on solutions requires system thinking along with system-based processes, goals, and metrics.

It may seem too obvious to state, but it is important to understand that products generally won't work well together unless the designer has designed them with compatibility in mind. Without stated goals of system compatibility, ways of measuring it, and processes that help develop and test for system performance, compatibility doesn't happen. It is the same with transformation. Transformation doesn't just happen by declaring a change; it is necessary to dig deep into the roots of the company. To understand transformation—where we are going—it is necessary first to understand the system that got us here.

Cause 2: Failure to Understand the Roots That Got You Here

Virtually every successful enterprise eventually takes what it was good at to begin with and re-aims the capability toward a different target. In 1920, IBM had a product line that included cheese slicers, butcher scales, and time clocks. Those items are still sold today, but not by IBM. That's because over the last century, IBM has been through three or four major transformations. CanCo, like IBM, faced a major set of decisions concerning how to focus the company beyond its dominant position in its current field. In the process, it came face-to-face with problems that emanated from its roots—what made it great in the first place. As you undergo transformation, consider your company's many roots, which may get overlooked in transformation because of the focus on the new product, service, or technology you're developing.

Root 1: The Core That Got You Here. What really drives meaning and passion in your company? This is the first question to consider in discovering your roots, and is also the first place to start redesigning in order to achieve transformation. What has the company been focused on that made it great? Was it a product, a service, or a contribution to society, or did it save the day for someone? What is the long-term extracted value that the company is dedicated to? Do people identify enough with your company that they use merchandise imprinted with the company logo? Why or why not? Answers to these kinds of questions help you understand what can motivate change.

If transformation involves changing or deleting any of the core items that are critical to how you got here, the scope of the effort to transform must change. At the same time, if there are things that made you great but that won't help in transformation, it will take careful planning to reorient employee passion. Consider the difficulty in transforming a company from start-up mode to scale-up mode when employees regard greater efficiency as the means of killing their sense of passion for unstructured exploration. What got the company here might be its explorers, but when it comes time to put in the railroad, the wrong crew is on board. The passion that got you here may kill the possibility of getting there.

Root 2: The Context That Got You Here. All companies looking to transform have a legacy context from which they operate. The context consists of all the systems, organizational measurements, goal sets, technology, structure, and strategy. Transformation implies a change in strategy and perhaps to goals, but what may get left out of the calculations is the rest of the context. What systems are central to transformation? What level of restructuring will you need? How will transformation change the technologies in the company? What new or altered measurements and information systems do you need for the transformation itself and for the transformed enterprise? When companies fail to answer these questions fully before beginning transformation, they can find themselves struggling to make changes. In CanCo's case, management discovered that the systems that had worked well to get products into channels did not work well when it came to getting solutions into accounts. In other words, the context that got CanCo here was killing its ability to get it there.

Root 3: The Capability That Got You Here. As we noted in the Introduction, four specific areas of capability are critical to transformation: portfolio management, program management, project management, and process management. When a company begins to engage in transformation, it is in these capabilities that cracks may begin to form.

Portfolio management is the process by which a company makes decisions about where and how to apply its human and capital assets. As an organization grows and develops, it learns to make decisions based on a complex array of factors. These decisions are heavily influenced by core and context elements. As a company transforms, the pattern of portfolio decisions must change. As resources are diverted from other areas into changing the business, the decision-making process needs to reflect this, and it is highly unlikely that a change in decision-making processes will happen without direct intervention. Without taking specific and direct control over portfolio management, an organization stands a high risk of making no change at all.

Program management follows the need for portfolio management. No matter what route a company took to getting to where it is, chances are that its strength does not lie in managing multiple integrated projects under conditions of organizational change. Transformation requires the management of multiple simultaneous projects, and implementing changes in products and services under transformation requires coordinated action across the entire organization. This means that HR will need to change the way hiring is done, Finance will need to change measurements, Sales will need a new skill set, and Service will need new systems. All of this spells program management as a central and critical need.

Programs are made up of projects, so success at program management requires capability in project management. Projects are work efforts that have a limited time and budget allocation to deliver something specific. With project management in place, the execution of the program plan under portfolio decision making becomes much easier. Having mature project management in place is a tremendous asset for an organization. Not having this capability may be a huge impediment to achieving transformation. Programs rely on project execution. Portfolio management systems don't work effectively if the project-level information in them is of low quality. If an organization is to transform, it must fill this skill gap.

The final capability is process management. Under transformation, many of the processes that have worked to get you here will now be a liability. Individuals form habits, and processes can become hard-coded (for example, airline reservation systems) or soft-coded (for example, how a person executes a task). In either case, processes must change. Transformation is difficult enough when processes are relatively well known and well documented, but when the process is embedded as tacit knowledge, change is much more difficult. Transformation depends on the ability to lead people through the pain and ambiguity of the change in capability that will get them from one model to the other.

Root 4: *The Competency That Got You Here.* The difference between capability and competency is the level of performance. An organization may have the capability to create a solution but lack the competency to create it at a high level of value. Capability gets you in the game. Competency is what allows you to win the game. Transformation puts all current competencies to the test. Some old competencies are transformable; some become relics. At one time, the competency to deliver 5.25-inch floppy disks was at a premium. Not anymore. In transformation, the old adage of "Know thyself" comes significantly into play. For companies that are extremely good at product design and manufacture, it is best not to assume that they can excel at creating a solution composed of multiple products and services. Part of this has to do with the development of new skills and talents for making the change from product selling to consultative selling. Some of the issue, however, originates all the way back to core. The marketplace sees a company and its brand as having a specific meaning. When a company makes a transformation, it may well alter that meaning in the marketplace. For a period of time, IBM marketed its Global Services organization as "the Other IBM." It took a branding campaign to begin to shake the product or "machines" image away from the solution side of the house. Competency does little good if the market cannot recognize, understand, and accept the legitimacy of the organization as it transforms. So one competency that is sure to get tested in transformation is branding. With APC, for example, its branding of "Legendary Reliability" can apply to products as well as systems. This is a big advantage. If your branding is centered on "We do chicken right," you'll find it hard to sell hamburgers.

Root 5: The Capacity That Got You Here. Transformation requires that the capacity of the organization change. Designing a solution where the delivery capacity is severely limited would hardly make transformation worthwhile. Given the right core modifications, context changes, engagement of capabilities, and development of competency, the capacity of the organization to grow the transformed enterprise becomes the key to extracting financial and human value. Organizations need to look at what they have had capacity for in the past and how they are going to create capacity in the transformed organization. Organizations must use efficient resource planning tools including competency considerations to determine what the shift of talent must be in order to scale to the transformed business model. Transformation is all for naught if it does not include the capacity to scale to the company's advantage.

Unfortunately, capacity in one area may not be enough if you are changing your business. In one company we are familiar with, the capacity to sell products was at a very high level. The strategy was to move to solution selling to bundle products in unique ways for the client. The resulting analysis showed that only about one in a hundred people who sold products well could sell solutions just as well. This is both a capacity and competency problem. The harsh reality is that transformation requires the right capacity of the right competency. The mix of capacity and competency that got an organization here may be what kills it there unless specifically addressed.

Root 6: The Customer Outcome That Got You Here. Great companies focus on what makes them great. They optimize certain outcomes for customers even if it means excluding others. For example, Apple optimizes the "cool factor" for its customers. In a recent advertisement for non-Apple computers, a person who is looking for a computer under a given price comes out of an Apple store empty-handed, saying "I am just not cool enough for a Mac." When you can get a competitor to articulate the customer outcome associated with your brand promise, that is as good as it gets. Although Apple does not use the word "cool" in its own branding, coolness is an outcome that it delivers to the customer. Consider how Southwest optimizes point-to-point flight economy and reliability, and Singapore Air optimizes passenger comfort and service for long transocean flights. These companies know the customer outcome they are trying to create and deliver on it. It is critical to transformation success that a company know what customers expect so that it can provide a better outcome or retain a blend of old and new.

The challenge for some organizations is in knowing what their optimized outcome is. For ALLDATA, the optimization point is credible repair data that lead to confidence in the estimate and repair quality. What is being optimized is confidence. If what got you here is optimizing confidence and what transformation does is threaten or modify the implicit agreement you have with your customers relative to outcome, that may be risking too much.

In the final analysis, whatever outcome is desired must be supported by and consistent with the context and core of the organization. This means that companies can't simply redesign the customer experience without looking at what is required to redesign the company from the inside out.

Root 7: The Culture That Got You Here. Corporate culture is hard to define and difficult to see directly. What people regard as culture is largely an expression of how they interpret the artifacts of behavior that form a pattern that is more or less unique to the organization. Numerous writers, scholars, and academics have pondered and published work after work on corporate culture, but many organizations are still left wondering how to change it. Our suggestion is to focus your attention on building or rebuilding core, context, capability, capacity, competence, and customer outcomes, and in the process, you will have modified all the necessary artifacts of culture that are pertinent to transformation. Starting the transformation process with a culture initiative is largely a waste of time because culture cannot be modified directly. It must be modified in the process of accomplishing something.

Consider, for example, the role of metrics in customer service centers. A call center might measure itself on call volume, problem resolution time, and time to answer. These metrics are internally focused and reflect a certain culture. The underlying problem customers face relative to call centers is that the product or service requires customer support in the first place. Few people look forward to placing a service call. What customers may want is fewer reasons to contact the call center. Therefore, a call center that is measured on driving down the call volume and call frequency will employ a different metric, such as the number of product or service issues resolved, which in turn drives a different culture than one that is focused on how many rings occur before the call is answered. Culture initiatives that announce "The customer is first" are largely a poster program unless organizations significantly modify culture through changes in context or other roots of what got them here.

Ambidexterity and the Challenge of Fundamental Change

You may find it tempting to retain the best of the existing business model while creating a new business model through transformation. The one that got you here is near and dear to your heart. The new one is where the future lies and where progress awaits. It is tempting to try to hang on to both. Forget it. The problem is roots. It is close to impossible to create a company that can simultaneously operate two distinctly different business models. Unless there is structural separation of some sort between the two, the roots of one will attempt to choke the other. We say that a fundamental decision must be made. If the old business model is to be preserved, it must be given room to continue to grow from its roots. Using structural separation, it is possible to create a new entity with a different set of roots. The other option is to modify the roots by orchestrating changes working outward from core. Do not attempt to create a combined root structure. Organizations, as is true of the people they comprise, cannot maintain two cores, contexts, capabilities, and so on at the same time.

Tune In to What Made You Successful (If You Can Figure That Out)

Pinpointing the exact cause of success can be as difficult as pinpointing the cause of failure. Studies have shown that people tend to ascribe success or failure differently depending on the outcomes they are achieving. If things are going well, conflict is seen as constructive dialogue. When things are going poorly, the same behavior is regarded as divisive. People ascribe causes after the fact. So if what got you here is a combination of things, it will take more than a casual survey to determine what it is that actually makes the organization tick. At APC, for example, technology, manufacturing processes, and the comprehensive distribution channel acting together made for a potent combination. These three things taken as a group appear to have had the greatest influence on APC's success.

In determining the reasons for your success, be careful not to confuse correlation with causation. Correlation shows that two items under study may happen in coincidence; it is distinctly different from causation, whereby a direct cause-and-effect relationship leads to the result. Organizations are complex systems, and to draw simplistic conclusions about what makes them successful is a risk to decision making moving forward. In considering what got you here and made you successful, ask yourself the following questions:

1. What basic motivating factor is the company widely dedicated to?

2. What long-term target or aspiration keeps the people in the organization engaged?

3. How strongly do people identify with a common image of the company?

4. How is the way you are organized conducive to success?

5. How have innovation and disruptive technology played a role?

6. What systems and processes deliver an inherent advantage to the company?

7. How has the company determined and met a clear goal set?

8. Is the way measurements are constructed an advantage?

9. Has the company created significant differentiation in the market?

10. How have investment decisions been made?

11. Are programs and projects run efficiently and effectively?

12. Does the company have a distinct advantage in process management?

13. What special skills, abilities, and competencies are strongest in the company?

14. Has the company maintained an advantage in scalability and capacity response to the market?

15. Has the company identified one or more specific customer outcomes to be optimized and delivered strongly on the brand promise?

Knowing what mixture of things got you here is critical in two ways. First, if you intend to keep the successful model in place, you need to know what factors cannot be destroyed in the transformation. Second, it is important to map the success factors that got you here to the required set that will get you there. To assume that what got you here is transferable is to pose a significant risk to transformation. As in the case of CanCo, it is a mistake to assume that if you have a strong sales organization that is successful in selling products, those same people can be as successful in selling solutions.

You can probably see that determining what made you successful will require doing some homework. Because transformation is a team sport, this task is best accomplished as a team assignment. Based on what the team finds, a composite sketch can be created for the face of change. Achieving a common understanding of the factors that got you here and those that will get you there is critical because it creates a "shared sense of the obvious" relative to decision making. However, you must take care to avoid group-think, whereby people are reluctant to voice their views because of the dominance and intimidation of people in the group or because of a faulty group process. It is important to get internal as well as external views. Also make sure not to succumb to analysis paralysis. Maintaining flexibility and momentum is more important than being totally precise.

Eliminate the Pathology of "Do It All"

Every organization must know its limitations. One of the most pervasive problems we have faced over the years is organizations' tendency to commit to action far in excess of their resource capacity. No matter how many studies are conducted and bodies of anecdotal evidence collected, there seems to be a deeply engrained madness in the executive suite, whereby executives fail to see the significance of resource management in transformation. If the leaders of a shipping company announced that their tanker fleet was to receive new hull structures while still transporting oil, they probably would be taken away in straitjackets. But many organizations in the process of transformation do much the same thing by attempting to change without adding resources.

What is needed is a strong decision-making system around redeployment of resources during transformation. The idea of multitasking and "working smarter not harder" is largely a fairy tale. Organizations struggle to find the resources available to make change, and when there is a lack of a critical mass of resources, the change fails. For example, if the sales organization cannot find the resources for developing new skills, the product development effort goes for naught because it dies in the sales process. If the sales process becomes fully capable of a new level of competency but manufacturing cannot deliver predictably, the change fails.

The key to eliminating the pathology of doing it all is the critical capability of portfolio management. Without it, decision making in the company is ad hoc and very risky. People begin to justify actions based on single-instance thinking, and integration of action becomes impossible to see and control. In the worst case, the lack of portfolio management creates a working environment in which it is difficult to succeed, which results in distrust and even resentment of the organization for not establishing clear priorities. If an organization does only one thing to initiate change, it should be the creation of the capability to execute portfolio management.

Unravel the Metrics

People do what they determine is in their best interest based on the payoffs of the game. The payoff can be tangible or intangible, but by and large, behavior is predictable based on the physical, emotional, financial, and psychological payoffs in a system. For transformation to succeed, the metrics that got you here must be evaluated for validity in relation to the transformation design. In one case, metrics for sales compensation began to get in the way of change. Salespeople who had been rewarded for large-volume product sales were less than enthusiastic about solution sales that had longer lead times and a lower probability of sales closure. Given the choice of selling products and getting compensated in the short term versus closing a riskier sale on a much longer term sales process, salespeople would inevitably choose the former. Self-interest motivates.

Metrics designed with a self-interest pattern that works against the way the company is transforming can be a major stumbling block. We are not talking about changing all the lag metrics of profit, revenue, earnings per share, and so on. What we are talking about are metrics that drive compensation, advancement, recognition, and actions leading to profit. If you think about a business from a process point of view, you can create in-process metrics that begin to shape behavior and therefore the transformation. If you try to simply create transformation without understanding the interconnected set of measurements in the system, you cannot change the organization.

Make the Whole Investment

There is little point in creating a thin veneer of change on top of a foundation that cannot support it. A business plan that positions the company as a provider of solutions is terrific, but if in reality there is no system investment, such a plan is a recipe for disaster. In companies we have worked with, it is not uncommon to find changes in the product or service stream that are not backed up by fundamental investments in the organization. To use a simple example, if someone gives us an indoor cat, we have to invest in a litter box, kitty litter, and cat food. If you acquired the cat without the support systems, you would have more than a few carpet stains.

Our experiences have shown that the following are some areas of investment that are likely to get missed:

- Core development for the rebranding of the organization
- The systems of context:
  - Measurement
  - Goal setting
  - Information
  - Reporting

- Internal communication
- Compensation
- Hiring
- Personnel development
- Structural changes
- Strategic planning processes
- Marketing systems
- Customer management systems
- Project, program, and portfolio management processes
- Training at all levels

Transformation does not come in a kit. The exact mixture of investments required for each company is unique: it varies depending on the nature of the transformation itself and the organization's current condition relative to the change. The most prevalent problem is the attempt to implement organizational change without mapping out the entire investment at least at a high level. Typically, transformation is attempted as a "must do," which blinds the organization from seeing that "must do" does not necessarily flow from what it currently "can do."

Summary

Michael Jordan, Charles Barkley, and Joe Montana all taught us a great lesson. Michael tried baseball, Charles tried golf, and Joe tried performance horses. Michael became a decent, but not world-class, baseball player. After a distinguished career as a basketball player, Charles is somewhere between a comedy act and a complete disaster with a golf club. Joe decided on performance horses after a Hall of Fame football career, but has not won any world championships as a horseman. None of them is world class in the area he selected after the one that "got him here." Organizations can learn from this. The factors that made them great in one area are not directly transferable to another area of endeavor. First, transformation requires a recognition that the change process is about the changing of systems, and sometimes individuals no longer fit the new system. Second, organizations must recognize the comprehensive roots of what made them great and be ready to deal with complex issues that may take longer to solve than the attention span or longevity of a CEO. Beyond that, organizations must be willing to dig deep to uncover what made them successful today if they are to understand how to redesign themselves for the future. To gain this perspective, it is critical to do the homework as a team. Trying to "do it all" will almost certainly end in disappointment, so a new or rejuvenated system of resource application must be put in place. Measurement systems can then be designed to emphasize the right things and reduce focus on things that don't matter, some of which were important in the past but have become irrelevant. Finally, the organization must be prepared to make the full investment or risk an incomplete change.

Ten Key Questions

1. Do you know what made you successful? How do you know?

2. What strengths do you have that are now liabilities?

3. What is the difference between your brand today and what you must make your brand stand for in the future?

4. How must the core of the enterprise change?

5. How must the context of the enterprise change?

6. What fundamental capabilities must the organization acquire?

7. In what way must the culture change moving forward?

8. Have you remapped the metrics to encourage the right actions?

9. Have you removed the pathology of "do it all"?

10. Have you made the entire investment in transformation or only part of it?

3

YESTERDAY'S LEADERSHIP SKILLS MAY PREVENT TOMORROW'S SUCCESS

Attitude is a little thing that makes a big difference.
—*Winston Churchill*

Bolthouse Farms is a fourth-generation farming company that started in Michigan and is now headquartered in Bakersfield, California. Bolthouse is a leader in its industry and a substantial and sustainable business economically, ecologically, and sociologically. It has a large share of the carrot market nationally and produces a line of beverages and dressings. In early 2009, Bolthouse Farms outsold Odwalla in its segment of the beverage market.

Jeff Dunn is the company's CEO. Jeff is not a native to the Bolthouse family. He came from different roots—he was the executive at Coca-Cola in charge of the South American region. After working at Coke for many years, Jeff came to his career-changing realization during a trip to South America. As he surveyed possibilities of how to expand the market for Coke in the region, he realized that the people of South America, who were lacking the basic infrastructure to regularly provide food, shelter, and sanitation, did not really need a Coke. Compared to the rest of the need structure, a sugar-based beverage seemed pale and perhaps the least of their worries. For a leader in a company that makes beverages of the sort that Coke excels with, this insight proved ominous and troubling. How is a leader supposed to create a new strategy and implementation for expanding into a market that he does not believe in? Perhaps one that he also considers counterproductive? This brought about a significant transformation in Jeff's life. He was faced with the choice between his spirit and his wallet. He chose his spirit. After separating from Coke, Jeff found Bolthouse Farms and is now running a company that he believes in on all levels. Jeff has gone through the process of transformation as a leader. He recognized the disconnect between what his job told him to do and what he could sustain as a person. He faced a tough choice and made the necessary sacrifices and calculated risks in order to make a sweeping change.

Jeff is a great example of what happens to people and organizations in transformation. Using his leadership skills to expand the market for Coke would have prevented him from creating tomorrow's success at Bolthouse Farms. (This story summarizes a presentation by Jeff Dunn at the 2009 Association for Strategic Planning conference.)

Leadership Lessons

People love stories like Jeff's because they turn out well. But they are also attracted to stories of the crash-and-burn variety for their trauma and drama. What is often missing is an explanation of the connection between what people do to succeed or crash and burn and what leaders should do in the leadership position they are in. The fact that Jeff Dunn succeeded or that Jeff Immelt is criticized by Jack Welch is irrelevant when leaders need to figure out what to do in their own situation. What is important is to understand the underpinning lessons at play and be able to apply those lessons to their benefit.

Lesson 1: Any Strength Used to Excess Becomes a Weakness in Transformation

Many leadership teams we have worked with are made up of individuals who are very strong and capable in one or more aspects of leadership. This probably comes as no surprise because, after all, how would these leaders have gotten to where they are if they did not have some significant stock in trade? But that is just the point. Whatever propelled the leader to a leadership position may now be a liability to transformation if those strengths limit or eliminate the opportunity for the leader and the organization to succeed in the future.

One team we have worked with serves as a typical example. This particular team had been assembled from people who share similar styles and preferences. These preferences led to a relentless focus on results as the preoccupation of their thinking, decision making, and navigation of the business. This focus isn't necessarily wrong, but there are three other aspects to consider when transformation occurs. One area of concentration should be creating a compelling vision for the future of the company. This team spent very little time and effort in this area. Second, there is the need to create intrinsic motivation through a connection to a deeply held purpose. The team had also spent very little time on this. Third is the need to cultivate relationships in the organization. This was probably the weakest part of this company. The net result was an inability to engage transformation on any reasonably effective level. Without the ability to articulate a changed organization through a compelling vision, engage the organization through intrinsic motivation, and create the relationships necessary to build teams of people to make transformation happen, the team and the organization made no progress.

Lesson 2: What You Don't Know About What You Don't Know Can Be Toxic

Leaders are expected to know everything at all times. Everyone probably recognizes this as an impossible standard, but it is difficult for many executives to consider their own blind spots. From the pedestal we place them on, leaders are treated as though they have almost limitless knowledge and wisdom. They know they possess no such property, yet admitting this would be a blow to their ego and power.

In transforming organizations, the number of unknown and unintended consequences can be daunting. If given too much thought, transformation efforts might become paralyzed. Yet leaders are reluctant to expose that which they don't know. More important, contemplation of the amount that they don't know about what they don't know is even less likely. An executive team we have worked with acquired a smaller company and, in the process, revealed that they suffered from a gap in their knowledge about talent retention. What they did not know about what they did not know was the unintended consequences of using monetary incentives to retain key talent instead of providing real and meaningful positions for the people involved. They assumed people would remain loyal if they were adequately compensated, but the leaders were wrong. This blind spot cost them a severe talent loss, which continued to hurt them as they misdiagnosed the reason for the loss, blaming the exit of talent on the weaknesses of the people who left. The remaining people in the organization recognized management's blind spot, but the continued ignorance of the leadership team resulted in a loss of their credibility and effectiveness. In this case, not knowing what they did not know was toxic to organizational talent.

Lesson 3: Your Beliefs Are Showing

The expression "playing things close to the vest" means keeping one's moves and motives hidden from view until one is ready to play the card at the appropriate time. This is perhaps a holdover from a time when business was more like a card game than it is today. People are far too sophisticated and aware of their surroundings and the moves of their leaders for this to be a useful mental model. So when a leader is mostly motivated by cash payout as a result of going public, or advocates "putting lipstick on the pig" as the way to sell the company, his or her attitude becomes obvious in less than a heartbeat to the overall organization. Leaders can lose massive credibility when they profess their dedication to the ongoing health of the business while at the same time folding their golden parachute for short-term deployment. The transparency of motives and beliefs goes far beyond the blatantly obvious financial incentives of the executive. A leader's beliefs on everything from the value of truth to the treatment of other people to what is in and out of bounds ethically are visible to the organization at all times. So even if leaders think they are holding cards close to their vest, they really hold nothing that cannot be seen in their actions.

As they approach the challenges of transforming an organization, leaders must take an inventory of what they really believe and what they really value, for in the process of transformation, they will be under an even stronger microscope, and their true attitude about the transformation will be transparent to the organization.

Lesson 4: Transformation Means Giving Up All Hope for a Better Past

Like the legacy ideas, systems, and structures we discussed in Chapter Two, leadership skills that got you here may kill you there. Yesterday's leadership skills created yesterday's results or today's results at best. These results are no indication that tomorrow's success is going to come from the reapplication of those same skills. Holding on to the good old days when your current stable of leadership skills worked successfully is the worst thing you can do.

For example, the ability to effectively produce in one's own technical discipline may be insufficient to handle the need to work across functional boundaries to produce an optimum solution for the business. Executives may have been spectacularly successful leading and managing a silo, but when it comes to being able to work collaboratively and cooperatively with a team of executives to optimize a solution for the enterprise, their skills collapse under the pressure. They make the mistake of creating suboptimized plans, taking an "It's not my problem" position when difficulties arise. We have seen engineering and marketing managers blaming others for the lack of sales performance of a product, when in fact those managers' commitment to an organization-wide solution was critical. Playing the blame game only made the situation worse, delaying the response of the organization to the market and thus deepening the problems. Thinking in silos and acting as an island may have worked on some level as a business grew and matured. But if the organization is going to transform, the silos have to be broken down, the leadership skills must adapt to an imperative of collaborative action and a move toward systems thinking, and leaders must give up all hope for a return to the good old days.

Lesson 5: Transformation Means Building Specific Leadership Abilities

Transformation requires leaders to shift their focus from what got them promoted and drove their bonus plan to what is going to preserve their livelihood for the future. The following are some of the competencies that leaders must cultivate in themselves and others.

Redesigning the Business Model. Leaders may know a great deal about how to orchestrate performance based on an existing set of key performance indicators, but can be less skilled at figuring out what the new service or product value chain needs to look like in the transformed enterprise. The ability to convert today's KPIs to tomorrow's is a discrete skill necessary for transformation. Also a part of the required skill set is the ability to redesign the organization from the outside in, on the basis of customer and market outcomes. Another is the capability to align the organization from the inside out, starting with the core aspects of the company. Creating strategy from the outside in while driving alignment from the inside out is critical for leadership teams.

Coping with Ambiguity. Transformation is messy and some-times frustrating. Patience and persistence are critical. Decisiveness is even more critical. Leaders are better off not letting their need for assurance become an excuse for inaction. Changing direction when in motion is much easier than when at a full stop. When it comes to making critical decisions in transformation, some leaders are prone to wait and see. However, there is no practical way to get every last detail figured out to a minute level of precision in making organizational changes. The leadership capability and competency to deal with ambiguity with a constant focus on purpose and direction are critical. The more ambivalent and indecisive a leader is, the greater the risk of creating an organization that is stuck in the transformation with no forward momentum.

Leaders must therefore increase their tolerance for not being sure. In the realm of innovation, a leader who is preoccupied by the notion of requiring absolute proof is not likely to lead anything significant. By the time there is proof, the opportunity to create something disruptive and differentiated is lost. This does not mean that leaders should throw caution to the wind and operate on the basis of gut feel and creative guessing. We advocate the use of evidence and discourage the demand for proof before action. Using evidence is about finding the indicators within data that are associated with trends and opportunities. Proof is a guarantee that any given course of action will absolutely work. To charge ahead without evidence is an accident waiting to happen. To stall while insisting on proof is looking for an opportunity for gain that will never appear until too late.

Altering Organizational DNA. Organizational DNA origi-nates in purpose, long-range intention, identity, goals, metrics, culture, structure, and strategy. Transformation requires the leadership skill to map the current organizational alignments, translate them into the necessary new alignments, and engineer the changes. It is simply insufficient to demand action from an organization that does not understand its fundamental execution DNA. Some executives get so wrapped up in driving action that they neglect the perspective and context of their own organization. Like it or not, economic crisis or not, market pressure or not, leaders must not abdicate their fundamental responsibility to put the organization in context for people and recognize the changes to DNA that are needed for the company to transform. When an organization moves from selling products to delivering solutions, it is easy to overlook the fact that the organizational DNA must be altered in the process. The goals of the organization, as well as its metrics, strategy, systems, technology, capabilities, and capacities, will all be different. Leading the existing organization in accordance with its DNA and leading the organization under a changed DNA are challenge enough, but leaders must also be able to lead *themselves* to transform. They must evaluate their own leadership DNA and be willing to change on a personal level.

Providing a Vision. We know what you must be thinking when you read this heading: "Oh boy, here we go with the mission, vision, and values discussion." Our experience would tell us that a soul-searching activity to find the perfect mission statement is largely an exercise in futility because at the end of the day, it creates another predictable statement about the treatment of customers, employees, and the community at large. It will probably be immortalized on plaques, banners, and Web site declarations and even printed on the back of people's security badges. Although there may be some value in all this, we have never seen any. What really counts is when a leadership team can make a case for change—articulate the message so that people know how to alter their course, their speed, and their decision making toward a new future. This requires a no-nonsense, high-clarity message delivered in multiple formats so that people understand the changes being made and can translate the message so as to answer the question foremost on their mind: "What do you really want me to do differently or better in order for me to succeed and for the organization to succeed?" If people are left with confusion about the nature of changes being made, fear, uncertainty, and doubt become rampant. Given the opportunity to fill in the gaps in leaders' communication of change, people will use their imagination. Leaders must be able to clearly state what situational factors are at play, explain what is changing to what, and describe what benefit is being created. It is also necessary to include an aspect of hope in your vision, which provides motivation. People undergo enough stress making things happen without the added burden of hopelessness.

Being Willing to Change Your Basis of Power. Leaders can base their power on a number of sources: their relationships with people, their knowledge, their control of scarce resources, or their ability to convince and coerce. They must recognize that changing the organization may require a change in their source of power. It can be a frightening thought for a control-oriented manager to consider that he may not be the one whose knowledge is critical to the transformed enterprise. If this leader has been in a position to coerce and dominate through the control of resources, transformation could cause him significant discomfort. The levers he used that worked in the past to generate influence may stop working. Leaders must engage in an internal transformation in order to retain, build, or reconstruct their power and influence in the organization.

The Insights organization, led by Andrew Lothian Jr. has developed a model that breaks the subject of transformational leadership into eight dimensions:

- Creating a compelling vision
- Communicating with impact

- Fostering teamwork
- Facilitating development
- Leading from within
- Thinking with agility
- Delivering results
- Leading change

Although leaders have the capacity to develop in eight dimensions, most leaders will be strong in some areas and less strong in others. If a leader has been very strong in delivering results in the current business model, this same strength may be a hindrance to teamwork and development. The opportunity here is to develop leaders who are more balanced across the leadership dimensions. Leaders must have the courage and foresight to lead themselves into a new level of capability by creating a more balanced set of leadership skills.

Exercising Empathy. People don't care how much you know until they know how much you care. That was the basis of Theory Z management three decades ago, and is still an issue in leadership today. One of the principles of change is the creation of a safe zone for people. Fear, uncertainty, and doubt create the risk of miscommunication, errant assumptions, and the chaos that goes with them. If leaders have true empathy for the people in the organization, they will create the best possible communication process for disseminating information about changes that are coming. If a leader lacks empathy, the organization will probably judge the leader as a narcissist and filter their listening accordingly. This can create a downward spiral of trust in the organization that hardens it to change. Leaders must examine their own motivations and viewpoint in order to maximize their effectiveness. In our experience, people are acutely aware of leaders who show no empathy, and treat them according to the level of evil they perceive.

Emphasizing Authenticity. There is an old axiom that states, "When all is said and done, there is more said than done." Leaders who say what they mean and mean what they say are in a far better position to lead transformation than those who do not. The degree of confusion or clarity in an organization is related to the leaders' authenticity. Those who engage in spin, half-truths, and vague communication are damaging their ability to lead the organization effectively. Trust levels drop as leaders demonstrate the gap between their outbound communication and their internal motives. Leaders must also recognize that their actions are a transparent way of analyzing their motives. Only by taking a rigorous internal inventory of their motives and purposes do leaders come to grips with who they are.

One of the main indicators of empathy in transformation is the treatment of people who are leaving the company. Some people simply need to change buses because where you are taking the organization does not fit with their plans or DNA. In cases where there is an honest mismatch between the organization and the individual, companies have a long way to go in demonstrating empathy. Meeting people in the lobby to prevent their reentry after lunch and turning off e-mail are common tactics to end the employment agreement. Aside from creating ill will between the ex-employee and the company, people who remain in the organization see the treatment that people get upon leaving and will expect the same treatment if it ever comes to their exit. They also know the true character of the executives who are responsible for the mistreatment of the people exiting. Nothing says more about an executive's level of empathy than the cruel and abusive treatment of people leaving the organization. In our experience, this is the most wasteful, morale-crushing, and inexcusable leadership shortfall of all. Leaders must reevaluate their treatment of people who are leaving as a result of transformation. It costs nothing to exercise empathy; the potential gain is the continued loyalty of the people who leave and the respect of the people who stay.

Cultivating the Ability to Make Tough Decisions. There is no transformation without making tough decisions in the face of ambiguity and conflicting information. As we've already noted, transformation requires an organization to part with legacy processes, people, and tools that have worked in the past but have no place in the future. Simply put, this is hard. We probably all know people who have hoarded everything they've ever owned, including the box it came in. The same can be true of an organization: it must change, but most people are reluctant to part with the past.

The first set of tough choices concerns people. Some of the people in the organization are your friends. Some have gone into battle with you. Some have made significant contributions to the organization. But none of these factors excuses a bad decision or no decision about the needs of the transformed organization. The leadership capability here involves the courage to do the right thing for the business and ultimately for the people involved even when it does not feel very good in the present.

If you have done your homework concerning what competencies you need and what the structure of the organization needs to be, you will have a much easier time making the decisions about people. That does not make it easier to tell someone that he or she is not part of the blueprint moving forward. It does not make it easier to tell a friend that the enterprise is not a place to continue the friendship.

The second major decision area is customers and markets. In order to transform your organization, you will probably have to cut some low-margin, high-maintenance, low-sustainability clients and markets out of the delivery model. As much as you would like to maintain customer service and retention, transformation means saying good-bye to customers that don't fit or cannot be transformed into the new model. Spirit Airlines and Southwest Airlines know exactly who they want and don't want even if that means taking some flak from the marketplace. Knowing what the new customer and market value chain are and what they are not is a major step in transformation. Sometimes transformation means shrinking the company in the short term to grow in the long term by focusing on a different customer and market. This may generate bad press, questions from stockholders, inquiries from the board of directors, and a host of other pressures. At the end of the day, the question is whether the leadership team has the capability to generate high-quality decisions about customers and markets and the fortitude to stand behind their decisions.

The third major area of tough choices is the use of resources. Many executive teams we have encountered over the years are afflicted with the notion that their organization can do everything they can dream up. Although most organizations have some system to deal with executive idea overload, few follow any process for accepting or rejecting ideas on the basis of available resources and other projects in the pipeline. This process has a name: portfolio management. With it, organizations can create a union between thoughts and actions. Without it, they are forced into a best-can-do position on an ad hoc basis. More and more organizations are embracing the idea of portfolio management, but many are still in the dark ages when it comes to employing true resource management to complement their visionary leadership.

Learning to Play the Part. If an organization is to be a solutions organization, it cannot act like a products organization. If leaders keep acting in the same way they always have, they are not signaling real change to the organization. There is no way to get big by acting small. On many occasions, we have encountered leaders who want to cling to the comfortable ways they have conducted themselves and their teams. This delays transformation. Some leaders resist processes and tools and offer such excuses as "We are not big enough for that" or "Our business is not that complicated" or "Everyone already knows how to do that" or "We can implement that when we are bigger." Clinging to the past without acting for the future will derail or delay transformation. Leaders may complain about organizational resistance to change while failing to address their own need to change. Leaders need to examine their own level of courage to let go of some of their self-limiting beliefs.

Increasing Problem-Solving Acumen. Transformation generates problems by the score. Cropping up during the process will be a myriad of problems that stem from unforeseeable impacts of changing the organization's business model. If the organization has no skill base in problem solving, major delays and frustration will result. Most people think of themselves as good problem solvers. After all, when they were in school, they did problem solving for twelve to sixteen years or more of their education. So they think they are part of an organization that knows how to solve problems. This is a mistaken assumption. What we have noticed is that organizations are often hampered by poor processes for identifying problems, analyzing root causes, engaging in action planning, and following through. Leaders in transformation must realize that the types of problems that show up are systemic in nature and cross-functional in scope, and probably touch on not knowing what the organization does not know. One of the jobs of the leader is to create a more sophisticated level of problem-solving capability than has been needed in the past. When problems that are rooted in systems across structures come up, the collaborative teamwork necessary to identify and implement a solution is far more complex than running the steady-state business model as it exists today.

In addition to engaging in classic problem solving, leaders must consider the limitations of the classic problem-solving model. Classic problem solving starts from a deviation that has a cause to be eradicated. A better approach might be to examine performance as a way to capitalize on strength rather than eliminate weakness. The field of appreciative inquiry has shown conclusively that some transformations are best driven from the amplification of strength as opposed to a concentration on weakness. Part of the leadership imperative in this area is to balance problem solving with appreciative inquiry to gain the best of both processes.

Leadership Diagnostics

There is no agreement as to form, format, or substance on the subject of leadership. Authors and consultants in this area all have some fundamental spin on the subject that follows a given philosophy or model. For Covey, the message is to apply seven habits and to be principle centered. For Kouzes and Posner, it is all about five fundamental processes of exemplary leadership. Although there is nothing wrong with these or any of the other approaches, there are fundamental gaps that they don't address in a straightforward way. Much of what is written about leadership is somewhere between happy talk and platitude. The following diagnostics are intended to push forward on the less discussed and most critical aspects of leadership that relate to transformation.

Do You Have the Strength to Listen?

Listening is different from hearing. Hearing is physiological. It is a function of the ability of the body to receive and process sound waves. If all the parts work properly, hearing can be tested using tones and amplitudes to verify basic functionality. Listening, in contrast, is psychological. If you break the word down to its parts, *psycho* and *logical,* what listening amounts to is letting in content before trying to make sense of it. We know that much of what the psyche decides about information is anything but logical, but the brain does not know that. The brain processes the physiological input through an elaborate system of biases and makes some sense of what is heard. The question for leaders is whether, given their own biases, they have the strength to listen to people. Biases are part of the human condition—we all have them. But some leaders have the inner strength to listen to things that raise red flags relative to their biases. Most don't. For instance, can you as a leader listen when

> The message is bad news?
>
> The ideas and suggestions are different from your precon-
> ceived notions?
>
> If what the person says is true, it will require significant deci-
> sions to be made?
>
> The message contains unpopular or politically charged
> content?
>
> The subject turns emotional or personal?

Listening under these conditions means quieting the internal voices of resistance long enough to hear what the person has to say. Many leaders' intolerance, impatience, and inner weakness prevent them from listening. This creates a leadership vacuum and limits the effectiveness of the leader. In transformation, a leader's ability to listen, diagnose, and then act is critical to leading the enterprise through transformation. No leader has all the answers. Some must come from others in the organization. Leaders who do not have the strength to listen are at a significant disadvantage in creating change.

Do You Need to Be Certain?

If the information concerning a leadership decision were perfect and complete, the course of action required would be obvious. By definition, decisions are made under conditions of uncertainty. We have seen leaders delaying decisions in the hopes that the uncertainty can be eliminated. As this is never going to happen, the effect is a continual delay of critical decisions. The consequences are many, including the impact of lost market opportunity, lack of focus, and dilution of effort across multiple initiatives in the business. A high need for certainty leads to an inevitable conclusion: making no decision is a decision. When we don't decide, we decide to turn the decision over to others in the marketplace and to chance. Letting others decide for us and throwing our fortunes to chance are not high-quality leadership practices, yet there is no shortage of this behavior in leadership teams. Leaders must examine their decision-making process and strike a balance between their need for certainty and the imperative of making a decision in a timely fashion.

Do You Need to Be Right?

Often wrong, never in doubt. That is the description many people use to describe their leaders. Leaders often require proof in order for them to feel certain, but the one thing many leaders are not in doubt about is how right they are. Whether they have reached their position through "proof by repeated assertion" or other means, the steadfast dedication to a position is typical of leaders. Much of the education we get in life focuses on getting the right answer, meaning a single unique and stand-alone answer. What is helpful in transforming organizations is the concept of multiple right answers. Leaders who can reach beyond thinking that they have the right answer open themselves up to possibilities for creative solutions. Transformation requires people to think in new ways and find new answers. A leader's preoccupation with being right will shut down the creative processes of people around the leader, create a dependency on him, and create a delay while people wait for the right answer to be given to them. Consider the cost of being stubborn. Do you really want to be right, or do you want to get results, transform the organization, and create organizational capability? Perhaps it is time to let others be right for a change. Perhaps you can try out new ideas instead of blocking them. This is not possible if you insist on being right.

Do You Need to Control?

It is possible to envision transformative change as a process that leads from a position of relative stability through a period of relative instability back to a period of relative stability. People are more comfortable in times of stability; thus transformation is about making people uncomfortable. The instability brought about by the relative ambiguity and the discoveries made during the process of transformation makes it almost impossible to maintain rigid controls. Further, it is possible that at the rate of continued change in organizations, the return to stability is largely a mirage. By the time an organization makes a significant change, it is perhaps time to make another. Considering these circumstances, leaders must be willing to accept the idea that their sense of control has to be replaced by a capability to influence. Some leaders are part of organizations that grew from very small teams; there was a time when they could more or less control what went on in the organization. But as span grows, control shrinks. The need to generate influence becomes the leadership imperative. There is no way to control the level of discomfort in the organization under transformation. Neither is there a way for a leader to control the actions of people under changing circumstances. If a leader defines herself in terms of her ability to control, transformation will either change or destroy her, or the need to control will destroy the transformation itself. Something will give under these circumstances. Leaders must consider

- The degree to which their self-image relies on controlling others
- How well they understand the difference between influence and control
- Where they stand in terms of their ability to empower others to perform
- Whether or not they can share power with others without feeling threatened

One could argue that control of organizations is a myth. Yet the number of executives whom we have encountered who strive for control suggests that it is a myth with many believers.

Clinging to control mythology limits executive effectiveness; and in transformation, exploding the myth is critical to executive effectiveness.

Have You Taken Time Out for a Hubris Check?

In his best-selling book *Ego Check*, author Matthew Hayward lays out 272 pages of research-based information on the destructive effects of hubris on careers and companies. Hubris can get in the way of reasonable decision making. In order to reduce their risk of succumbing to hubris, leaders must

- Consider the evidence on which their decisions are based
- Become aware of how many decisions they make that defy the evidence
- Seek out dissenting opinions
- Give risk analysis a fair hearing (and listening)
- Consider all the information without selective hearing (and listening)

Wishful thinking combined with too much caffeine, adrenaline, and other hormonal secretions is a dangerous mixture. Ill-conceived mergers, acquisitions, strategic alliances, strategic initiatives, and joint ventures can result from fuzzy thinking brought on by hubris. Executives who are open to examining their level of hubris reduce their risk of making a colossal error without reducing their chances of creating a spectacular success. Hubris only has a downside.

What Is Your Level of Narcissism?

Narcissism is a preoccupation with one's own gratification accompanied by blindness to the impact on others. Countless people have documented the relationship of the performance of the organization as a function of having something to believe in and a path to follow. For the narcissistic leader, the path toward his own gratification is the purpose of the organization. This goes beyond self-centeredness. In this leader's view, he is the reason for the organization, and all decisions are colored by his own wants and needs. When a leader becomes more interested in creating exit strategy than in creating sustainable enterprises, then stock options, bonuses, payouts, and going public dominate his thinking. His decision patterns give the narcissistic leader away because his decisions are made with short-term payback in mind. And the payback is designed to compensate the leader most generously.

Because their motivations are readily apparent to the organization, narcissistic leaders lose effectiveness and hinder organizational performance by undermining people's morale and sense of meaning in their work. We suggest that leaders examine their real motivational factors and include a narcissism check to go along with the aforementioned hubris check. If the organization is just a tool in a narcissistic game of self-aggrandizement, we suggest you take an inventory of the risks and rewards and rebuild your fundamental sense of purpose.

Do You and Your Team Have Real Self-Awareness?

Chances are that if you have been in business for over a decade, you have been through multiple self-assessment sessions in which you were given some kind of designation that was associated with your leadership "type." The problem with most of these systems is that they give you enough information to be dangerous but not enough to be operationally effective in driving improvements in the organization. Although many things in life can change, your natural tendencies are not one of them. The good news is that you can be profiled to the point of near-total predictability. The bad news is that if you were hoping to undergo an extreme makeover—leadership edition, it is not happening. Unless we experience a life-changing event, we do not fundamentally alter our approach to the world. This means that we have inherent strengths and inherent weaknesses, which allow us to contribute as well as to make mistakes.

Operating from strength while not honoring and compensating for weaknesses is a bad risk management strategy. Many executives are willing to take credit for their brilliance but not for their blind spots. When executives recruit others in their own image, they form a team with a collective shared blind spot or spots. In transformation, this shared blind spot—a case of the blind leading the blind—is the biggest risk factor in formulating change. Add to this collective blindness a case of hubris and a dependence on being right and certain, and you have the perfect mixture to ensure that the organization is going nowhere quickly. Executive teams need to get some help with understanding styles and preferences. Despite the risks and resistance to action in this area, self-awareness can be the biggest payoff for executive teams driving transformation.

Is This Really Your Thing?

This is the slippery slope of the leadership discussion. The business model that requires transformation may have been a masterful creation by the existing team of people, but that does not mean that they have the ability to create what is next. Between the golden handcuffs of current salaries, bonuses, and stock ownership plans and the fear factor associated with making a career move, executives can get into a self-made trap of continuing when they should be exiting. Some characteristics to consider in the process of deciding how to engage the challenges ahead are leaders'

- Level of passion for change
- Degree of determination and perseverance
- Willingness to make sacrifices
- Ability to make unpopular and difficult calls

- Dedication to sustainability
- Motivation grounded in sustainability

In our experience, this is the discussion that needs to take place that rarely does take place. It would be great if all leaders had the capability to move past all the obstacles to transforming themselves and their organizations, but there can be a fundamental disconnection between the competency level of the executive team and the requirements of engaging and orchestrating change. Unfortunately, the realization that there is a massive misfit among the competencies on board may well occur after the transformation is in progress. Therefore, this might be a retrofit exercise that resembles in-flight kite repair. We don't know of a preventive measure in this regard. The issues must be a matter of some degree of discovery—with one major exception: one can predict the executive team's blind spots. Leaders can identify the resulting risks and take action to head off the largest issues related to the blind spots in fundamental leadership capability. There are good ways to get this done if the executive team will embrace the need to evaluate their collective weaknesses and take action to mitigate the associated risk.

Summary

Transformation puts significant stress on leaders and leadership. There are significant risks in what leaders tend to do in transformation that are brought on by the ambiguous and messy nature of transformation. The five lessons and the set of diagnostics we've offered here are a start to getting a better handle on leadership development for creating transformation. Some of what we have said is likely to be a bit disturbing and maybe even confrontational. The problem we have seen in our work is that these are the issues that need to see the light of day and get worked on directly, instead of being swept under the rug in a form of denial. The issues we raise here are not going away without direct effort on your organization's part to produce better leadership practices and better leaders.

Ten Key Questions

1. What is your point of view on leadership? Does it match the reality of the challenges you face?

2. What leadership strengths from the past are now weaknesses?

3. What new leadership competencies are critical to your transformation?

4. Where are your potential blind spots in terms of leadership competencies?

5. What changes are you willing to make in leadership to be successful in transformation?

6. Do you have superior listening strength?

7. What is your tolerance for ambiguity?

8. Have you specifically looked at the level of narcissism in the organization?

9. Do you and your team have solid self-awareness? How do you know?

10. Is the transformation of the organization really your thing?

4

THERE IS NO STRATEGY IF NOBODY KNOWS WHAT TO DO

What to Do with a Complex Strategic Agenda

Allen is a project manager for a global company that installs major infrastructure projects, such as roads, dams, bridges, and pipelines. His current job, which is in South America, has been running quite smoothly up to this point, but he has just been informed by a local government official that there are a few safety problems with his project's operations that could become problematic. The official gave Allen two options. The first option requires a three- to four-month delay and will push the project into a cost overrun due to late delivery. The second option is to pay the government official a sum of $100,000 in small unmarked bills, rendering the problem harmless. What should Allen do? He has signature authority for sums greater than $100,000, so he could create a phony invoice and pay the official. If he doesn't pay the official, he risks the consequences of delivering late, which he knows will limit his career in his company. But by paying off the official, he risks everything he has worked for his entire career. Allen has to make an important choice that will have significant strategic impact and serious consequences. Which way will Allen go? How do you know?

The reality of executing strategy is what people do day by day, hour by hour, and choice by choice. Whether they like it or not, organizations are almost totally at the mercy of what people decide to do or not to do. Shad Helmstetter once pointed out that there are thousands of choices in a day, and all of them count. If your organization has thousands of people, then there are at least a million choices in a day for each thousand people you have. In addition, all of these individual choices must support the corporate strategic choices as to whether to enter markets, create new products, or implement new systems, or the corporate strategy fails.

Part of the challenge of implementing strategy at the individual level in the organization stems from the fact that it hasn't always been an issue. There is not a long-standing history or body of knowledge to guide the translation of strategy. During the time when the world was largely agrarian, strategy was dictated by the farm owner. People who worked on the farm followed the owner's directions in terms of when to plant, what to plant, when to cultivate, how to water, and when to harvest. Alignment in this case meant that either the field got plowed or it did not. In the industrial era, alignment was also relatively straightforward. If someone in a factory was not making choices consistent with production (such as by putting a wheel on an axle), it was obvious. People are either assembling the product correctly or they are not. But that was the end of simplicity in strategic execution.

Fast-forward to the information age and the age of the human network. The simplicity and transparency of the individual choice have disappeared. If someone is doing intellectual property work that requires creative thought or collaboration of teams, the connection between the individual's work and the larger corporate strategy is not directly observable. Although this has always been true of people doing knowledge work, the difference today is that a much larger percentage of the people in the organization are knowledge workers. How these workers choose to spend their time, effort, and energy is not obvious, so it is harder for management to know whether individuals understand and are acting in accordance with the strategy of the organization.

Our experience tells us that people struggle to understand how their organization's strategy, as it has been communicated, translates to what they should do at their level. Under these circumstances, their options include the following:

1. Taking their best guess based on their own criteria and agenda
2. Ignoring the strategy-speak and doing what they sense is best
3. Pretending they understand by converting conversations into buzzwords
4. Doing nothing while continuing to report progress
5. Asking for clarification at great peril of being branded as someone who "doesn't get it"
6. Doing some combination of all of these

When we have thousands of people making thousands of choices, this can become wasteful at a minimum, catastrophic at a maximum.

A Case in Point

A company we will refer to as SparCo was two years into an effort to deploy a change in strategy and had met with limited success. SparCo's product line was challenged by competitors who could produce products for personal and small to midrange applications at a lower cost. In light of this, SparCo's new strategy was to defend its product-based business while adding a totally new business model to capture emerging opportunities in the large systems area.

SparCo struggled in rolling out this new strategy for a number of reasons. First, not everyone in the organization knew the details of the strategy. Only a select few people in SparCo had seen the strategy documents. As a result, there was no unified understanding of what to achieve by when by whom. In addition, there was no master plan for execution and little portfolio control over the investments needed to make the transformation.

In order to make the strategy work, SparCo needed to execute a number of major changes that required the alignment of all aspects of the organization. First, it had to successfully create a new SparCo brand for its large systems solutions, while maintaining its brand as trusted adviser and product producer. Essentially, this meant shifting from a brand as just a product producer to one as also a business continuity provider. In addition, market share erosion for its products had to stop (exactly how was not documented), and new roles, such as embedded systems engineer, had to be created—all without substantive change to the structure of the company. Under these circumstances, consider the situation of a salesperson who has to make choices every day and is now being asked to sell both stand-alone products and integrated solutions. Here are some of the factors this salesperson might consider:

- SparCo is branded as a products company, not a solutions company, so I need to do a lot of positioning work for solution sales.
- For a given customer, the person who buys detail products is a different person than the one who builds systems.
- I am not trained as a systems engineer, nor do I have such a person in the sales process with me at all times.
- A product sale is largely a single-stage transaction with a long repeat business trail.
- A solution sale is a multistage transaction with complex contracting, a long lead time, and a lower probability of payoff, and is largely a project-based sale that has an end.
- Commissions for products are short term; commissions for solutions are long term.

  Question 1: What choice is this person likely to make as to how to spend his or her time?

Question 2: What is likely to get sold under these circumstances?

Question 3: What happens to the strategy of "business continuity supplier"?

Answers: (1) The salesperson is going to be creating product sales. (2) Products. (3) Dead on arrival.

To deal with this strategic complexity, SparCo had to translate the business strategy so that the entire management team could understand and deploy it. The leaders needed a way to simplify the message so that it could be disseminated throughout the organization in a consistent manner. They began by explaining the business model for products and solutions, which consisted of five application areas and four basic channels. Because the customer outcome differed between selling products and selling solutions through all channels to all application areas, this meant that SparCo's strategy was made up of forty discrete elements (4 channels × 5 application areas × 2). Establishing a basic business model that everyone could understand allowed for conversations and questions and a greater understanding by employees of what part of the matrix was being discussed. A turning point occurred when the organization realized that each one of the forty pieces of the strategy contained a slightly nuanced customer outcome. Basing the organizational strategy on these customer outcomes helped make clear what needed to be done to optimize business performance.

After this realization, the executive team spent eight consecutive days immersed in the strategic planning process, which is unprecedented in terms of executive commitment to clarifying strategy. As a result, the executive team converted the strategy into actionable elements and created a coherent portfolio of projects and programs necessary to execute the strategy. Their initial planning work allowed for a cascading set of planning sessions that disseminated the strategy throughout the company.

Lessons in Strategy Communication

Working with the executive team at SparCo provided us with a number of important lessons regarding how to make sure that people know what the organization's strategy is and what they should be doing in support of its execution.

Simplify the Message

Many salespeople have heard the statement, "The confused mind always says no." In other words, if you confuse the customer, there will be no sale. When we talk about organizational buy-in, we are actually talking about something similar to a sales process. People don't buy in to a strategy that is not communicated in a simple and understandable way. This means they don't own it either. The goal is a simple, but not simplistic, strategy. Simple is great, but simplistic creates an environment suitable for a "Dilbert" cartoon. One approach is to take your existing strategy and break it down into three categories:

1. Things you are going to do more of
2. Things you are going to do less of
3. Things that are going to remain about the same

At the end of the day, strategy does not consist of anything more than these three aspects. Everybody needs to know what to increase, what to decrease, and what to maintain. If people can get this message, their decision quality will improve, and so will strategic execution.

Focus on Outcomes

To avoid a lot of strategy babble, focus the conversation on the optimization of specific customer outcomes. A common error in strategic planning is to focus the strategy on revenue growth, market share, new markets, and globalization without necessarily understanding how the business model optimizes specific outcomes for each individual customer constituency. In the case of SparCo, the customer outcome varied by channel, by application area, and by the difference between products sales and solution sales. So when the company was formulating its strategy, it had to account for the differences among various parts of the overall model. Among other things, this type of focus will reveal problem areas in the organization—those areas in which employees must choose between two diametrically opposed outcomes to do their job. If we consider the example of the SparCo salesperson, we can see that the salesperson is being forced to choose between the optimization of his or her own commissions and the expansion of solution sales that is strategically critical to the company's future. Unless compensation plans or organizational structure is altered in support of the strategy, the strategy for becoming an enterprise continuity provider falls on its face. If the strategy is so complicated that the connection between the strategy and the organizational structure, organizational goals, measurement systems, and organizational culture becomes obscured, there is little chance of being able to translate the strategy to every organizational level where people can make supportive and effective choices.

Get to Clarity Through Immersion

Everyone is busy to the point of distraction. Most people have at least two cell phones or smart phones. Considering text messages, e-mail, voice mail, and phone calls, the attention span of the average executive is now about thirty seconds. Coupled with executives' predisposition to be extroverted thinkers, this phenomenon can lead to attention deficit disorder at the strategy level. There simply is no substitute for a strategic planning process that allows people a reasonable amount of time to understand what they need to do to execute strategy.

Although immersion in a process doesn't guarantee success, there are ways of improving the odds of getting the message across to people in a meaningful way. People receive information in three primary ways: visually, auditorily, and kinesthetically. Visually, people need to see information through pictures, diagrams, models, and charts, and are influenced significantly by the use of color. (In one case, we encountered a CEO who takes in information almost exclusively visually; any e-mail to him longer than five sentences is largely a waste of time because he cannot and will not process it.) So it is helpful to produce visual representations that convey the direction of the company. Auditory people need access to quantitative data and written information. For many people, it is critical to be able to read the details and receive information in the form of text and numbers; they rely on that type of information to formulate their understanding. Without this level of detail, they have no way to translate effectively, and strategy is therefore largely lost on them. Last, an important lesson we've learned over the years is that there is no substitute for physical involvement in activities that are used to formulate the strategic plan. The physical writing of notes, the physical creation of charts, the physical interaction of people in the process are powerful means of absorbing the strategic message. If you doubt the importance of the combination of visual, auditory, and physical involvement, try teaching a four-year-old how to tie her shoes over the phone when she is in the middle of a soccer game. You will have about the same amount of mind share as you do trying to get your point across in most of your meetings.

In order to reach the visual, auditory, and kinesthetic threshold of real understanding of a strategy, teams of people need to meet face-to-face. Although organizations may be reluctant to invest the time and the travel and logistics costs of face-to-face, colocated planning, consider the cost of ineffective strategic execution. When the opportunity cost and loss risks are considered, a short, well-designed session can be, by far, the lowest-cost option. We ask that executives consider the affordability of having the strategy derailed by the lack of effective communication. What an immersion process does is create a solid common understanding so that the strategic message does not get lost in translation.

Cover All the Bases

Psychologist Carl Jung, among others, suggests that there are four main ways in which people translate an abstract concept, such as strategy, into an action, or what they need to do as a result of that strategy. First among them is the need for people to understand the action plan. People in this category are looking for dates, places, speed, urgency, tangible things, and events. Part of the strategic plan and strategic planning process must address the need for people to understand goals, objectives, metrics, key performance indicators, business value, return on investment, profit potential, market share, market size, timetables, and roles and responsibilities.

Second is the need for socialization. People's need for connection leads them to form relationships, which are often referred to as social networks. Social networks are a much more powerful tool than the lines and boxes of the organizational chart. When people understand their place in the organizational structure through a social network lens, they can begin to find themselves in the organization and understand how they relate to others. In order to communicate strategy effectively, it is important to be aware of and utilize an organization's social networks. We often hear people discuss strategy in terms of "If that is our strategy, who are we?" What they are really asking is, How does the strategy relate to how we are connected and who we represent collectively as an organization?

The third aspect of translating strategy into action relates to inclusiveness. What are the implications of strategy in all parts of the organization? People are curious about who is affected by changes and in what way. They're concerned about the impact on relationships within the company, between the company and its customers, and with general stakeholders. The major concerns are who is affected, how are they affected, and whether the strategy is deployed fairly.

The fourth way in which people translate strategy into action is through their consideration of facts and figures. To be able to interpret strategy at the local level, people need to see the charts, graphs, spreadsheets, tables, and written descriptions. Sometimes we refer to people who relate to information in this way as bean counters. The reality is that these people provide a critical service to the organization by making sure that the math and the logic follow the rhetoric. Without them, organizations can turn factoids—which have the appearance of truth but no data to back them up—into facts and treat them as truth. In the next meeting you attend, make a mental tally of the number of times people cite things as if they were fact when what they are really expressing is an opinion.

If we are successful in communicating strategy in a way that integrates these four needs, we have a much better chance of maintaining continuity between the actions taken by a planning group and those taken by the people in the organization as the strategy is deployed.

Use a Full Set of Tools

To create strategic plans that can be communicated to the organization effectively, it is critical to use all the tools and processes at your disposal. Listed here are a few of the things we've found really useful that also satisfy the four ways in which people translate strategy into action.

Goal Maps. Most people have heard of strategy maps, but few have ever used a goal map. Goal maps visually connect an organization's internal and external commitments over time to the work required to deliver on the commitments. Here is how it works: a team of people lay out the target achievements for an organization in time sequence. The target achievements can be expressed in terms of product releases, service releases, events, profit levels, revenue levels, and so on. Once the team has agreed to the target achievements, they connect the projects required to meet the goal to each specific goal or achievement. The team can also identify the key performance indicator and key predictive indicator that can measure success toward the completion of the goal. In a relatively short period of time, a team can create a goal map that includes a measurement system for navigating completion of a goal by tracking the work associated with achieving the goal.

Strategy Maps. Strategy maps have been around awhile, and most often are used incorrectly. Strategy maps that start with the financial aspect on top and track the internal perspective, customer perspective, and learning perspective are really built inverted. The subprime mortgage disaster is a perfect example of what happens when the focus is on ROI and not on the customer outcome. By providing loans to people who had no long-term ability to service the loan, banks put too much emphasis on short-term financial scorecards and too little on a sustainable customer outcome.

A more effective strategy map starts with customer outcome at the top, adds the competitive approach as a second layer, identifies critical systems as a third layer, and identifies the critical resources required as the bottom layer. This way, the organization does not lose sight of customer outcome as the central element in strategy formulation. When people understand the desired outcome, they make more intelligent decisions about how they can help produce that outcome in the best possible way. In organizations that have not done a rigorous job of strategy mapping, there exists a high probability that the organization does not fully comprehend how value is really created inside the business. This lack of comprehension limits people's ability to choose their actions in alignment with strategy. Having as many people as possible to engage in the process of strategy mapping at all levels of the organization is a critical and powerful way to create coherent strategic choices.

Causal Loop Diagrams and Interrelationship Diagrams. There is a critical lack of systems thinking in most executive teams. Many decisions are taken in isolation using a low-quality decision-making process. Causal loop analysis and interrelationship diagrams graphically show the relationship between reinforcing and countervailing elements in a system. By developing an understanding of the interrelated elements of strategy, people can begin to understand how the business model works and to improve their decision quality. These diagrams are a powerful way to communicate strategy in a consistent way across the organization and make the work of strategic planning more portable as people leave strategic planning sessions and begin to deploy strategy through actions that they take.

Process Maps. You may be wondering what process maps have to do with strategic planning. As it turns out . . . a lot. One of the biggest problems in the process of formulating strategy is a lack of accounting for the system's capability to support the strategy. As crazy as it seems, in transformation, companies often overlook the fact that their fundamental business processes were designed to support a product strategy and are ill-suited for the change. People make choices based on what the systems will allow them to choose. Proposals, sales, customer service, marketing, compensation, customer records, and so on are all systems that could support the old business model but maybe not the new one. If you haven't included a thorough business process mapping of the implications of change, the strategy could get derailed. Process maps help you ensure that the overall investment in strategic change is included in the portfolio.

Use Portfolio Management as the Control Point

Everything an organization does to translate strategy requires some sort of an investment. Every piece of work that is identified in the process of strategic planning boils down to an investment of time, effort, and energy. These investments must be comprehended by the portfolio of projects and programs that deliver strategy. When portfolio management systems are constructed correctly, the priority of the project within the portfolio reflects its strategic value. In many cases, however, the portfolio has a prioritization scheme designed around return on investment or net present value; such a scheme makes it difficult, if not impossible, to trace the value of the project to strategy. Creating portfolio management systems that use goal maps, strategy maps, process analysis, and causal loops to pinpoint the strategic value of the project gives you two distinct advantages. First, you know what a project will deliver and how that benefits the strategy associated with your goals. Second, if you decide to make reductions in the organization, you base your decision about what projects to remove on what alterations you make to your goals. Quite often the portfolio management process and the strategic planning process are disjointed, leaving individuals in a quandary as to how to operate under the guidelines of the portfolio while striving to support the strategy. If the strategic agenda of the company is controlled by the portfolio management process, the portfolio becomes the control point in transformation as well.

Maintain Continuity Between Planning and Action

Six months after a strategic planning cycle, most organizations have lost the ability to track the initiatives that they launched with regard to the desired set of organizational goals they set for the year. The organization has no way to understand where additions, changes, and deletions need to be made to navigate the organization to transformation. By this point too, it is hard to see the causal relationship between the existing project portfolio and the transformation of the organization. This is because most tools and systems are not designed for forward and backward traceability. When you establish your strategic plan, you need to make sure that the systems capability associated with portfolio management includes forward and backward traceability so that you maintain the capability to navigate your transformation, make changes, and add and remove work. Without this capability, neither the organization nor the individual can make coherent choices.

Communicate 5-by-5

Simply posting a strategy document on a network drive or attaching it to an e-mail won't cause much to happen in terms of spreading a transformational message and plan. Choices in the organization will be largely unaffected. Many people point to communication as a significant issue in their organizations. Ask any group what their major problems are, and the word "communication" will show up in the top three items. Although communication is commonly named as a culprit, we have found that teams do very little about it. If the term is defined as pure input, there is no shortage of communication to most people. The cell phones and smart phones we carry provide a nonstop stream of communication. The real issue is whether the information being received is pertinent or not. If it shapes choices in the right way, it is pertinent.

As we outlined earlier, people take in information through three basic channels and in four preferred ways. Just as brand recognition requires about eight exposures before it begins to take root, people are not going to "get it" on the basis of one communication blast. Communicating 5-by-5 must be part of the strategic plan. The best way we know of to get a message across is to use five methods of communication at five separate times; methods can include the following:

1. E-mail
2. Automated voice mail

3. Webcast

4. Webinar

5. Town hall meeting

6. Podcast

7. Newsletter

8. Discovery map (such as those produced by Paradigm Learning)

9. Video conference

10. Video download

11. Prepackaged presentation

12. Dedicated Web site

One size does not fit all.

Summary

At the end of the day, strategy is implemented because of the pattern of choices people make in the course of doing their job. As an organization grows, it becomes much more difficult to influence those choices. Sometimes choices become embedded in rules and processes so that individuals have limited choice. If every business model worked like McDonald's, where the menu is under strict control and the transaction is push-button driven, transformation would be much more straightforward. Because that is not the case, you need to immerse your team from top to bottom in the process of strategic execution. The process must honor the way people take in information and provide the kind of information they need to make effective choices. You are far better off if you use a complete tool set in the creation of plans. Communicating five times in five ways is the best assurance that people are going to get the message in a way that sticks and that shapes the choices in the organization. Communication is one of two hygiene factors. The other one is follow-through from planning efforts. Maintaining the link between the brainstorming activities, the plan formulation, and the taking of action is critical. The chasm between an off-site and strategic execution is large and full of best-laid plans. Finally, you must maintain traceability from the work to the goal set so that you can make changes in an agile manner. Transformation requires a new level of sophistication in strategic leadership and management.

Ten Key Questions (Plus One)

1. Can your organization state your strategy consistently in plain language?

2. If you ask five people at random what the company strategy is, will they answer consistently, coherently, and correctly?

3. What is the success rate of your projects? How do you know?

4. Is your strategy more than a statement of financial measurements?

5. Has the team been immersed in strategy, or was it handed to them?

6. Are you willing to invest in ensuring that strategy is deeply understood in the organization?

7. Has the strategy been translated into an investment portfolio of projects to make it happen?

8. Are the resources available to accomplish the strategy? How do you know?

9. Can you draw a picture of your goals and strategy freehand on a single piece of paper? Can your team do the same?

10. Do you have a way of tracing strategy to goals to measurements to projects to tasks and back again?

11. If you had to take a reduction of 20 percent, would you know what to cut so that you minimize the impact on your goals?

5

TRANSFORMING STRATEGY REQUIRES MORE THAN EXPENSIVE SOFTWARE

A tool without sound processes will make you a fool
with a tool

—*Mark Morgan*

Today's project portfolio management (PPM) systems can track hundreds of projects across thousands of people, provide cost tracking, and produce more reports than a staff of a hundred people could read, let alone act on. What these PPM systems won't tell you is whether the project should have been done in the first place and what would happen if you simply stopped the project and saved the costs associated with it.

There is a good reason for this, of course. The makers of the tools and the creators of the reports are responding to the need to create a tool, not to the need to create the business intelligence to use the tool to maximum advantage. The tools do not help you calculate strategic value. The tool can only respond to the numeric value placed in a field. How the number was derived is a totally separate matter.

The plot gets a little thicker when we delve into the question of why the tool companies do not have a solution readily at hand for how to derive strategic value. Apparently, very few people are motivated to engage the organization in a conversation about where the process for making such a determination resides. In one case, we interviewed a major tool provider and asked what its PPM tool got used for in a typical installation. The answer was that customers are using it for registering projects into what is known as a project registry. That is the rough equivalent of buying a supercomputer to do nothing but keep a grocery list.

But to tread into the arena of why certain strategic choices are made is to walk on thin political ice. A dirty little secret of organizational life is that the decision making behind product launches is analogous to monetary decision making made in a politician's home district: decisions are made behind closed doors, using logic and reason that are not widely shared. Transparency of process and decision making is typically not a priority, and when the status quo is disturbed, strong forces come into play to protect the system in an "as is" state.

Why would major stakeholders not want more transparent decision making? Let's consider their motivation:

> *Executive management.* Some executive teams do not welcome the accountability engendered by transparent decision making, so the idea of creating specific, disciplined decision criteria to be used inside the portfolio system can be far from attractive.
>
> *The tool supplier.* Most tool suppliers have little or no organizational expertise in creating strategic priorities, nor do they want the capability. If tool suppliers can make a sale downstream of strategy, they would be nuts to bring up anything that would jeopardize that sale.
>
> *The consultants.* Much like the tool suppliers, they sell to the executives who are not strongly motivated to transform the decision-making process. Consultants do not want to create enemies in their account and are therefore not motivated to ruffle any feathers by asking embarrassing questions and proposing radical changes that threaten the power structure. No consultant in her right mind would knowingly open an issue that has more risk than return for her.

The project management office. At the point where a PPM tool is needed, the PMO is probably drowning in the process of trying to track projects and get some form of resource reconciliation in place. These people very often lack the skills to carry on the discussion over how to populate the strategic value field. Just like the tool supplier and the consultants, the PMO goes by the old saying, "Never miss a really good chance to keep quiet."

The strategic planners. Although the planners have the strongest motivation to get strategic value translated into the portfolio, they are typically not the ones driving the installation of PPM. The typical motivation for PPM is to get control over the project world, not to ensure that strategic value is extracted from the project world. Therefore, PPM ends up being deployed into IT as a means of sorting projects across the stakeholder community.

Given all these reasons why key stakeholders are not motivated to change the decision-making process, why bother? The fact is that transformation cannot happen without inserting strategy into the decision-making pattern. Although it is a messy change, it is critical that the leadership team open the discussion around what is strategically important so that the tool sets and processes of project, product, program, and process development that are central to transformation can be executed. Judging from what we have seen, there is a clear need for organizations to take a closer look at the shape of their decision-making system and consider a significant upgrade in organizational capability. Many organizations have low or no maturity in their ability to make a clear, well-defined decision on where effort and resources that support transformation should be placed within the organization. The process that holds the greatest promise for the organization is portfolio management.

Educate the Executive Team
on Portfolio Management

As much as they would hate to admit it, many leadership teams do not understand the basis and the benefit of portfolio management. In much the same way they have been doing budgeting for years, many organizations simply ignore the opportunity to show traceability from goals, metrics, and strategy to the programs and projects that deliver them. Portfolio management benefits the organization by

- Establishing a link between the stated direction of the organization and the actual work being performed
- Allowing for clear priorities that get the organization mobilized on the basis of a common understanding of what comes first
- Generating accountability throughout the organization for targeted results
- Clarifying where to increase, decrease, or eliminate resources in real time

In the short term, portfolio management allows for greater alignment of resources with strategy, greater clarity of direction, and improved processes to determine priorities. In the longer term, it promises to be the best bet in preventing the type of problem that we see today, as automobile companies crumble from their previous status as icons of industry.

The executive team may struggle with an understanding of portfolio management. Although some of this struggle will be due to the change in mental models represented by thinking in these terms, much of it will be related to the levels of transparency and accountability that portfolio management demands. In portfolio management, the decision process is made more transparent—that is, the whole organization will be able to see what decisions are made and why. This transparency then leads to greater accountability. Chances are that if you have attempted to implement portfolio management in an organization and the "culture" killed the effort, it was really a mortal fear of transparency and accountability that was at the root of the resistance. Overcoming this problem is critical and a matter of education, patience, perseverance, and gut-level determination.

Think "Just Enough" to Prevent Overkill

We suggest that rather than signing up for some large tool deployment, organizations establish their ability to rationalize the decision-making process starting from the foundational concepts of the transformation, before trying to implement microscopic controls. In other words, "macro leadership" must precede micromanagement. The reason for this is to establish a balanced set of criteria that can be used as a decision-making framework. This basic framework can be put in place without a huge tool implementation. Once the framework is in place, the larger tool implementation can be used to become very precise about the deployment of resources. Getting the process right will get you in the right ballpark relative to decision making. A tool deployment applied to good process can provide the automation and precision to improve efficiency. No tool can overcome poor process. In this area, you need to think about process first and tool second.

Integrate Portfolio Management and Business Process Flow

Once upon a time, the world moved slowly enough for the annual budgeting process to suffice in shaping direction. That was because substantive changes in the environment that required changes in an organization's course were slower than the budgeting cycle. But coincident with the advent of Internet speed, annual budgeting could not keep up with the pace of real-time changes. Today, transformation requires day-to-day diligence in shaping the decision-making process. A critical capability in executing transformation is in establishing a framework for decision making that can shift resources in real time based on the changing landscape of business. Without this connection between the changing environment and how the organization uses its resources, the organization ends up with high-level decisions that lack the action where it counts to create results.

In one organization we worked with, there was a need to create a decision-making framework for selecting markets and opportunities within those markets. The organization faced a situation where more opportunities existed than resources to exploit them. The pipeline of opportunities and the deployment of resources were compared to the desired balance of risk and return. The result was a healthy reallocation of resources away from imbalanced areas toward an optimum balance. Essentially, this created a connection between the strategic direction of the company and the actual work being performed. It also created a means to decide what the work of the organization should be, before inappropriate work had a chance to take root. This process has not only earned the approval of the board of directors but also created a much better risk-adjusted portfolio for the business with a minimum of complexity and cost.

Get Clear on the Real Drivers Behind the Business

The idea of *efficient frontier*—that there is an optimum mixture of investments that will yield maximum benefit at a given level of expense—has been around for decades. (See Figure 5.1.) It was originally used, for example, by oil companies in considering the relative value of a large assortment of drilling locations. PPM tool suppliers attempt to make the point that the concept of efficient frontier applies to the project environment in your organization. The basic argument is sound, with one catch: you have to know what drives strategic value in your business, or there is no way

Figure 5.1 The Efficient Frontier

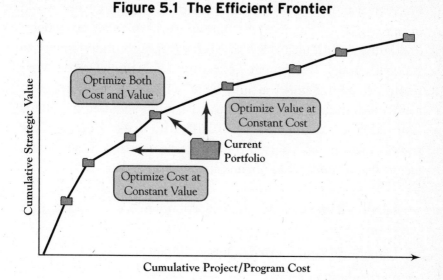

Cumulative Project/Program Cost

to create the vertical axis of this chart. Whether you end up using the concept of efficient frontier or not, the imperative to determine what drives strategic value in your business does not go away. At any given level of expense, there is an optimum allocation of resources or mix of projects that corresponds to a level of strategic value. But knowing that this is the case does not do you any good if you do not know what drives strategic value in your business. No matter what you spend on software, it will not be able to tell you what your value drivers are. That is your responsibility.

Transformation also requires you to be specific about what fundamental aspects of strategic value are being preserved, discarded, or added. It further requires that more or less weight be placed on those criteria that are more or less influential in decision making. If all of this makes you want to go back to gut feel, and to hell with the idea of trying to figure out how to make a better decision, don't feel alone. Most organizations are not naturally disciplined about where to put their resources. It is a bit like the day we realized that mom and dad were not going to fund us forever, and we had to figure out how to pay our own way in the world. Growing from the adolescent world of narcissistic behavior to the mature world of balanced budgets and living within means is a tough transition for individuals and is equally tough for company executives. Getting clear on what really drives the business and what will drive transformation relies on discipline—much like the discipline required to emerge from adolescence. In order to clarify the driver necessary for transformation, ask yourself the following question: *What are the factors that account for the organization's success?* Was it

- Supply chain efficiency, design, dominance, exclusivity, and so on?
- Distribution network size, design, alliances?
- Vertical integration?
- Defensible market position through differentiation?
- Brand power?
- The overall solution offered?
- The creation of a system or platform?
- Intellectual or emotional appeal?
- Product or service features, function quality or performance?
- Service?

In answering this question, ask yourself these two additional subquestions for every response.

1. How do we know?
2. What do we have which shows that to be the case?

These questions will help you avoid confusing whether results are correlated with drivers or caused by drivers. For example, if you think that you are successful because you provide excellent customer service, you need to ask whether excellence in customer service is causal to your success and, if it is, how you can show it.

Without asking these two questions, you don't have any evidence, so you are liable to see one as the cause of the other, when in fact there may only be coincidence (correlation). Correlation is not causation, and transformation must deal with causation. Correlation will come later.

Ask yourself this question as well: *What are the future drivers of success that represent transformation?* Are they

- Control of scarce resources?
- Defensible technological position?
- Solving more of the customer's problem?
- Channel partners?
- Consultative solutions?

The same two subquestions—How do we know? How can we show it?—become critical here as well. Think back to 2004 and consider what it would have taken to prove the value of Twitter. Chances are that the transformation you have in mind is not as radical as this, but there has to be a theory of operation that drives the decision process. In order to execute the Twitter or Facebook level of radical change, an organization has to shape decisions to optimize social network appeal, rather than succumb to the typical net present value or return on investment myopia that pervades some company thinking.

Link Projects to Goals

Vertical integration of resources to goals is one of the most challenging undertakings for an organization. Yet if you do not have this linkage, there is little or no reason to expect that your goals are going to be reached. Undisciplined processes allow poor decisions, which allow behavior that is misaligned to goals or allow goals that can divert resources. The linkage required is as follows (Figure 5.2):

Figure 5.2

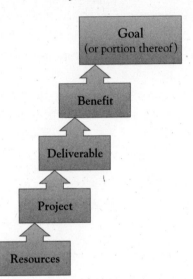

This relationship diagram reflects the link between the resources needed to accomplish a project with a specific output that creates a benefit that satisfies a goal. Creating such a diagram seems simple enough until you realize that most goals are so generally stated that you wouldn't know how to reach them in any predictable way. In other words, a goal is reached as a function of the sum of the projects that bring it about. If the projects are designed and executed with the whole in mind, there is less waste and greater performance.

Take Decision Making Beyond ROI

When organizations lack the process for linking higher-level concepts to the work going on in the trenches, portfolio decisions are often made based on return on investment (ROI). This is unfortunate because simple ROI calculations are typically no more than numerically expressed guesses dressed up as precise analytic conclusions. Using ROI as a discriminator is insufficient to create transformation. Having wrestled with and succeeded in determining the factors that lead to organizational transformation, we have learned to create factors for selecting investments and using resources that generate balance between numerical values and less tangible factors in the decision-making process. These factors that need to be considered in portfolio creation are

- Emphasis on purpose (discovery, heroism, altruism, excellence)
- Long-range value to stakeholders
- Brand impact
- Contribution to goals
- Impact to key metrics
- Cultural acceptability
- Economic, social, and environmental sustainability
- Level of innovation
- Extensibility (ability to make another move after this move)
- Length of exclusivity in the market

Companies facing radical change must balance their portfolios by looking at how much of the portfolio is devoted to keeping the lights on (working in the business), how much is devoted to improving existing aspects of the business (working on the business), and how much is devoted to moving the organization onto a different plane (working to transform the business). Chances are that if the portfolio is heavily loaded with working in the business, there is little organizational capacity to truly transform. Without creating balance in the decision making and balance between working in, working on, and working to transform, transformation will remain stuck in the mire of resource contention. Just enough portfolio management is the best way to get unstuck.

Develop Decision-Making Expertise

Most leaders consider themselves good decision makers, but we have seen numerous instances of poor decision making at critical junctures. Part of the problem is the tendency of organizations to focus on decision rights rather than right decisions. Decision rights are a matter of power and politics in an organization. Some people consider the autonomy of making decisions as the reward of organizational power. But no matter where the decision rights reside, the quality of a given decision is a function of the process used to make that decision. It is also important to note that decision quality does not guarantee a correct decision. This can often be difficult for leaders to understand, as they expect a high-quality decision to be the same as a "right" decision. A high-quality decision does not guarantee a positive result. Many organizations praise people for decisions that have positive results, whether or not it was a high-quality decision. This approach is contrary to building organizational strength. What helps build organizational strength is training, coaching, and mentoring on the process of making high-quality decisions.

There are six steps in making high-quality decisions. (These steps are adapted from John Celona and Peter MacNamee, *Decision Analysis for the Professional*, 3rd ed., Menlo Park, Calif.: SmartOrg, Oct. 2001.)

Step 1. Frame the decision, as in "What are we really deciding?"

Step 2. Generate creative, doable alternatives.

Step 3. Gather and use the most reliable information available.

Step 4. Engage in clear, rational thinking (even if it is outside the box).

Step 5. Apply clear values and tradeoffs.

Step 6. Commit to action.

Transformation requires that you rebuild the organizational patterns embodied in steps 1 through 5 and follow through with meaningful action. The goal in transformation is to reframe decision-making patterns, change the alternatives you pick from, change the basis of your information, alter the thinking pattern, modify your value and belief systems, and change the actions you take. By doing so, you are changing the culture dramatically. If you can create substantive change in how high-quality decisions are made, you have a good chance of making transformation happen.

Create a Neutral Third Party

When organizational capability is low and there is a significant gap between the current state of affairs and desired performance, we recommend a modest amount of centralization. Many organizations resist this for a number of reasons, but organizations need a nonpartisan influence whose sole purpose is to drive decision quality and to link strategy to the portfolio of projects and programs. Here we outline a few ways to help create change that serves transformation.

Implement a Central Office

Call it a Strategic Planning Office (SPO), Strategic Execution Office, Office of Strategic Management, Office of Strategic Execution, or whatever you like. The main thing is to put in place a small but influential group that owns the processes of strategic planning, including the rationalization of resources. Give this group the authority to determine where the organizational capacity limit is reached. Consider creating responsibilities that include

Strategic planning
Competitive analysis

Portfolio management

> Defining the execution process
>
> Tracking and reporting of strategic execution
>
> Creating and tracking the strategic execution budget

You must ultimately base the design of your central office on the unique needs of your organization.

Focus on Project Management Capability

One of the sure signs of poor project management capability is the use of spreadsheets or slide decks for scheduling. When Microsoft people say that the biggest competitor to MS Project is Excel, they are not kidding. Many organizations have so little appreciation for project management methods, processes, and tools that they would not see the significance in the first sentence in this paragraph. After decades of training, consulting, and professional accreditation, many organizations lack the simple capability to plan, organize, track, and manage projects effectively. As a result, they struggle with strategy execution and the inability to get the information they need to improve. Portfolio management depends on project management for demand and capacity information. Leaders must take the initiative to understand the project management world well enough to know that each project represents a packet of their strategy and to take it upon themselves to improve the process by which these packets are delivered. Project management is a strategic competency.

Implement Using Internal Champions

Transformation is not a good time or place to subcontract or outsource the implementation of critical processes. Consulting firms can help immensely, but they need internal champions and sponsors to succeed. The line executives must align behind the necessary changes, or the results will be false start after false start.

In one case, an executive implemented portfolio management by starting in a single section of the business and using that experience as a means of dislodging resistance in other areas of the business. Consultants helped create the framework of the portfolio management system, but it took continual internal influence from a line executive to eventually push the concept across the organization. It is often much more effective if the internal champion uses outside resources in a coaching and mentoring role rather than in a central role in making the change.

Summary

Co-dependent agreement is a psychological term used to describe situations in which people agree not to discuss a subject because it is too charged. Whether we like it or not, many organizations have co-dependent agreements in avoiding discussion of the link between the strategic agenda and affordability. Although there are good reasons why nobody is motivated to come forward and take on the nasty job of intervening in a dysfunctional system, intervention is sorely needed, and transformation depends on it. Linking strategy to action is a huge step in creating the ability to transform. What is being sought here is what is contained in the Thunderbird Professional Oath of Honor:

As a Thunderbird and a global citizen, I promise:

I will strive to act with honesty and integrity,
I will respect the rights and dignity of all people,
I will strive to create sustainable prosperity worldwide,
I will oppose all forms of corruption and exploitation, and
I will take responsibility for my actions.
As I hold true to these principles, it is my hope that I may enjoy
    an honorable reputation and peace of conscience.
This pledge I make freely and upon my honor.

The best way to increase the honesty and integrity of an organization is to ensure that the ideas of the company are reflected in the decisions the company makes at the portfolio level. This practice also ensures the inclusion of all stakeholders in decisions, sustainability, responsibility, and accountability, and ends corrupt and exploitative practices by making the decision process transparent. If the people running organizations are willing to take the Thunderbird oath and live up to it, implementing portfolio management could be a natural step instead of an area of dysfunction.

Ten Key Questions

1. Has your organization installed a tool or system in the absence of a process that utilizes the tool effectively? (Have you become a fool with a tool?)

2. Does your organization suffer from system overkill for the problem at hand?

3. Do you have lots of data but no real information?

4. Does the executive team understand portfolio management?

5. Have you linked projects to goals?

6. Do you have a balanced and comprehensive decision-making system that goes beyond the obvious ROI criteria?

7. Do you have a strategic execution office that centralizes control over low-maturity processes?

8. What is the state of your project management capability?

9. Do you have internal champions who have the influence to create real change?

10. Are you willing to take the Thunderbird oath?

6

TRANSFORM HUMAN RESOURCES INTO A STRATEGIC ADVANTAGE

> I am perfectly aware that HP has never guaranteed
> absolute tenure status to its employees; but I also
> know that Bill and Dave never developed a
> premeditated business strategy that treated HP
> employees as expendable.
>
> —*David Packard*

In a small meeting, several executives and a consultant sat discussing the situation facing the future of their business. The company was losing its competitive advantage due to its outdated technologies. The mood was somber—if the company did not start generating revenue from new products and services, it was in severe jeopardy. These changes meant a significant shift in capabilities and competencies, most of which were undeveloped in the company. All of these changes involved a change in staff. The team recognized that they had great athletes, but the game was about to change dramatically. Some of the people that had been A players were not going to maintain that status. New skill positions would be needed, along with new people to fill them. These new positions would also involve new hiring processes, performance planning, job design, and work on organizational structure and culture. Realizing that these changes would require a strong Human Resources department, the consultant asked the executives how they felt about their HR organization. The executives' eyes rolled back in their collective heads. This was their weak spot. At this critical time in their transformation, HR was not up to the challenge. All that HR delivered was low-level administrative support and enforcement of rules.

This is not an isolated case. In fact, it is more the rule than the exception. In general, the HR function has been underdeveloped and overlooked as a source of strategic advantage. In a recent article, for example, consultants from Booz Allen Hamilton listed ten questions that they consider critical to mergers. One of the ten questions asks about talent attrition; the other nine focused on non-people-related issues, such as markets, operational integration, and so on. What makes it worse is that the metric that is implied in the talent attrition question is "How many people are we going to lose?" Why not ask, "How do we make sure that we retain all the relevant talent that makes this merger a valuable one for all concerned?" ("Making the Most of M&A," strategy+business, Summer 2009: 72). When it comes to transforming organizations, a company's talent is an integral component of net worth, yet it does not get equal billing with financial considerations in the design of M&As or the creation of strategy. Although there are multiple reasons for this lack of understanding on the part of business leaders, failing to have a trusted HR partner with a respected voice is one of them.

Develop HR in Two Stages

If transformation is to succeed, HR must play a critical role, meaning that HR must be a full partner in the strategic plan and execution. But how do you do this when you do not have the required skill set in the HR department? For many companies, solving this problem occurs in two stages. The first stage entails dealing with a less than fully equipped HR organization; the second stage involves motivating businesses, academia, and professional associations to cultivate a new level of integration between the HR function and the rest of the company. In this chapter, we address both stages.

Stage One: Filling the HR Gap

Many organizations face the situation described in the beginning of this chapter. They recognize that the level of HR support they need does not exist in their organization. Between the acknowledged shortfall in skills and the real blind spots caused by not knowing what they don't know, organizations can get very frustrated with the human resource challenges associated with transformation.

There are quite a few capabilities needed to rise to the transformation challenge. First, the organization needs new competency models. The reason for this is uncomplicated yet seemingly difficult for many leaders to enact. If you do not clearly define what you or the customer needs, you will not be sure when you find it. The competencies required for product sales are different from those needed for solution sales. Our experience tells us that less than 10 percent of people who are good at product sales can successfully sell a solution. Although some can make the transition, most cannot. Further, an underperforming HR department may not even recognize that the organization needs this new competency—a situation where they don't know what they don't know. The organization also needs new hiring processes. If the hiring processes are not changed, the company culture will not change, which is a necessary part of any transformation. Organizations can encounter the same problem here as with competency models, in that their HR department may not know what they don't know when it comes to bringing new talent into the company. HR in isolation will struggle with encouraging misplaced staff to move on to other opportunities more suited to their capabilities in the newly transformed organization. Leadership needs to cooperate in "changing the management." People who have been A players in the business over the years may be only C players in terms of the transformed company. This is where a competency model is invaluable. The agreed-on competency model allows for mature, objective dialogue to take place with these employees about their performance and to do so based on the predetermined needs of the customers. Without taking the time to think about and establish new competencies, there is little chance of success to rework the leadership into a transformed state.

New positions, new competencies, and new hiring processes also mean new compensation structures. People do largely what they get compensated to do. Deming is credited with asserting that defects are caused by systems that compensate people for creating defects. If the company has been designed to compensate for unit sales and the transformation calls for system sales, the compensation system needs to change. HR must be fully engaged as a strategic partner if this change is to be successful.

Along with new compensation structures, the organization will need new performance measurement mechanisms. Transformation demands a change in performance management, which means that the company must establish new criteria by which to measure that performance. People who have settled in to performance measurement systems under an outdated model must be realigned to a new set of performance standards, and possibly even a new job description. HR and line management must work in tandem for this change to take place.

HR cannot make all these changes in a vacuum. While HR drives the human asset inventory, it has regulatory constraints to work within when doing so. Leadership needs to provide clarity about the business model in order for HR to do its job effectively. HR effectiveness is limited by the weakness of organizational leadership. The level of resolve for transformation in the leadership team is another factor that can either support the strength of the HR role in transformation or become a limiting factor. The executive team needs to articulate a clear rationale for transformation and show commitment to it. This means stating specifically what the transformation entails, why it is necessary, what benefit is being achieved, whom it will affect, and what success means. This is a prerequisite to getting full engagement from the HR community. Without a clear transformation rationale, HR is in a position akin to pushing a rope. The executive team cannot expect HR to work against a fuzzy agenda.

The executive team, along with HR, also needs to clearly establish the strategy associated with transformation. HR depends on the clarity of the strategy to formulate the competencies, capacities, and capabilities of the organization. The question of "who" is interdependent with the questions of "what" and "where." Jim Collins asserted that to get from good to great, it is necessary to get the right people on the bus and then figure out where to go. Unfortunately, sometimes we look around and find out that the bus we are on is full, with all the seats taken up by incumbent employees. Once HR knows where the bus is headed—what the shared strategy of the company is—it can reload the bus with new and retrained people. Fundamental to creating clarity of strategy is identifying what the customer outcome will be once transformation has occurred. Worthwhile transformation is not likely to occur without designing strategy around the customer outcome in multiple layers of the profit value chain.

In the process of transformation, ideas are going to be flowing, people will be exploring alternatives, and the opportunities for conflict are sure to become plentiful. It is important for the executive team to be aware of their own preferences, communication styles, and sources of conflict in order to operate with speed and efficiency. Here too, HR skills are needed to manage the personalities, "blamestorming," rumors, and other dysfunctional behavior that accompany change. Profiling instruments and other tools and processes are often useful in understanding and providing a remedy to these problems. This ability to create relationships among the different people and personalities who can effectively make the decisions required for transformation is a rare but essential element in the HR equation, and the use of tools, such as

Insights™, will assist the executives in navigating what can be very turbulent waters.

In stage one, where the on-board skill of the HR organization is not up to the task, the organization requires an infusion of resources to break the logjam and move forward on transformation. The required infusion must come from outside the organization, which presents a few options. One option is to bring in a new HR team. Chances are that the existing team in the organization has its hands full dealing with the administration of hiring, termination, salaries, and benefits, which is important and needs to be executed. Our experience of most HR departments is that there is no slack present, and without slack there cannot be change or a lot of time for strategy development. If the competency in the HR team has not been developed or invested in beyond administrative tasks, it is time to bring in new talent and to begin investing.

Another option is to get some help for the HR team you have. If the problem is mostly a lack of HR capacity to take on transformation, bringing in additional staff to take the pressure off of the existing staff could free up enough resources to make a significant difference. When there is no slack in the HR function, expecting them to take on transformation is nothing short of cruel, as well as largely ineffective. If you need to act quickly, you may also consider using an outside firm to advise you in HR matters. This approach may have its own share of problems, as organizations need to be very clear on what consultants can and will deliver without creating a dependence on them. Before you hire a consultant, first consider the cost of not transforming. If the relative cost of the lack of change is low, there may be no justification for the cost of a professional services solution. However, if the reality is that the company cannot afford to wait, so to speak, the cost of bringing in outside support could be in the best interest of overall performance. In the long term, the organization should recognize that having an OD professional on the HR team is essential because the reality of business is that change is constant.

Stage Two: Building HR Strength in the Long Term

What HR Organizations Need to Do to Develop HR as a Strategic Partner

In *Chicken Soup for the Soul*, the author tells the story of Dr. Glenn Cunningham, who as a boy was injured in a fire that damaged his leg function to the point of a near-death experience. He was lucky to survive, and the doctors thought he would never be able to walk again. Ultimately, Cunningham set a record for the one-mile run.

In some ways, this story of triumph over difficult circumstances is the story of HR. Currently, in many organizations, HR does not have fully functioning "legs" relative to transforming organizations. Because HR tends to get branded as an administrative function, its value as a strategic partner is "operationally challenged." In talking to HR professionals around the world, we saw clearly that HR's transformation to a true business partner is exceptionally difficult. You can expect to hear hallway conversations along the lines of "The department is not going to make it" and "We might be better off if HR was completely outsourced" or "Do they really know what they're doing?" There will be days when even the strongest of HR leaders will question whether or not the day-to-day struggle is worth it. The resistance to an HR department positioned as a strategic player on the team appears in many forms.

For example, you can expect questions to fly the first time the sales team hears that a member of the HR department wants to go with them on their next sales call: "Why does HR want to be on a sales call with me?" "Did I do something wrong?" "What do I tell the customer?" "Should I start looking for another job?" Responding with "HR is working to become a strategic partner to the business, and as part of the process, we are working to understand the business" can elicit reactions ranging from complete skepticism to genuine excitement.

One of our most telling experiences came from a change we orchestrated in how an HR team we worked with related to the customer of the organization. HR team members were assigned to go with the sales team to customer meetings. Both salespeople and customers thought this was highly unusual, but were willing to engage the process. It became necessary for the HR professional to explain his or her presence at a sales call. The explanation went something like this:

> Mr. Customer, thank you for taking the time to meet with us this morning. I am from the company's human resources department, and as part of the transformation of HR within our organization to become strategically partnered to the business, we are out talking with customers directly. We strongly believe that in order for us to be hiring the A players to meet your organization's needs, we have to hear directly from you. HR inside our organization must understand what is keeping you awake at night. It is only then that we will be successful in not only hiring the right people but also structuring our organization correctly to serve you.

This explanation allowed the customer to become very comfortable with the presence of the HR person and allowed the salesperson to focus on the call. What was gained in the process was an increase in the understanding of customer viewpoint within the HR community. This is critical if HR is going to take a more systemic view of the organization, a crucial part of being a strategic partner to the organization.

But this transformation will not happen overnight. It will happen one day at a time, one conversation at a time, one individual at a time. As a profession, HR has been quietly, or sometimes not so quietly, in this state of transformation. Inside of most forward-looking, progressive organizations, the HR professional has played many roles: a coach to managers, an architect or adviser on new organizational designs, a truth serum when the leadership team needs a reality check, a talent scout on the lookout for A-player talent. This is not easy! It requires a lot of humility and humor. And the business leaders who are now partnered with these HR professionals would have it no other way. For these leaders, regardless of their chosen profession, market segment, language, culture, or rank, there is no going back to the old role of HR. The value is clear, and HR as a partner is here to stay.

The time for transformation is now. Although it can be painful and can look very ugly in the middle, it is something that must be recommitted to every day. That is how someone like Dr. Glenn Cunningham becomes the fastest runner in the world.

There are a few ground rules for those attempting to grow HR into a strategic partner role. First, you need to get the basic administration done before you can realistically have a discussion about working as strategic partners. When the fundamentals of dealing with people entering, exiting, and performing in the organization are not in place, HR loses credibility and cannot step up as a strategic partner.

Once credibility is established, HR professionals must understand what organizational strategy is and what it is not. Strategy consists of a mix of activities that are intended to create added value to the customer and build value in the business. With a grounding in goal setting, strategic planning fundamentals, and strategic execution, an HR professional can be a value-adding partner in creating strategic options and avoiding strategic blunders due to people-related constraints.

Once HR understands what strategy is, it needs to be clear on its organization's particular strategy. When the strategy is in the executive's mind and nowhere else, HR needs to be brutally honest. With HR's help, executives need to make the strategy tangible and translatable into simple terms. Why? So that HR strategy can be aligned with the company strategy. If the company strategy is based on supply chain efficiency, the HR strategy needs to reflect how the people in the organization are being developed to deliver supply chain efficiency. This might seem trite, but it is amazing how many times we see little direct connection between HR strategy and business strategy.

HR has been the target of criticism for a long time, but respect cannot be gained when there is less than an A player in the game. The organization needs to staff HR with A players in order to get A performance. There is no way to create A-level performance with C players.

Respect from line organizations also comes when HR people know the business they support. HR professionals must have an in-depth knowledge of the work that people do within their support envelope. If you have HR people supporting manufacturing, put them into a rotational assignment in manufacturing as well as with the suppliers and customers of manufacturing.

Last, don't forget the humility and humor. Here is an example ripped from the pages of our experience. In one case, an HR director was asked how things were going in one of the company locations in Asia. The director replied that there were some potentially "explosive" issues, but everything was going to work out fine. Shortly after, the HR director was called to report on the status of a *factory explosion* in Asia! The lesson here is that we all have to take responsibility for words that don't translate well or can be misinterpreted. Hence, humility. But at the same time, it is important to appreciate the comedy of situations that are the base material for cartoons. HR is a difficult arena and often has the disadvantage of dealing with a large portion of not-so-good news. With humility and humor, the HR professional is much more likely to contribute in meaningful ways and much less likely to burn out.

It's Time for Professional Associations to Change

Much of today's HR functions stem from the industrial era. During that period, the labor force was largely fungible, meaning that people could be replaced on an assembly line with relative ease because work was compartmentalized and largely repetitive in nature. HR was needed only for hiring, salary and benefits administration, and regulatory and legal compliance. Today, the demands are much greater. Employees are knowledge workers who are much more difficult to replace.

The educational programs of the Society for Human Resource Management (SHRM), "Business Education for HR Professionals" and "Executive Education," are a step in the right direction. SHRM's certification courses serve HR professionals well and are a response to an obvious need of organizations across the world. In a time when for-profit and nonprofit organizations are struggling to deal with challenging economic realities, CEOs and boards of directors are searching for ways to identify HR professionals who have both the experience and the education to assist them in transforming organizations. Some of the ways to meet the challenges for HR include the following.

1. **Develop a senior executive forum.** A high-level forum is needed where senior executives exclusively can have an open dialogue with senior HR professionals about the challenges they are confronting. Most executive-level business leaders do not come from HR. Most are technical, marketing, or sales oriented. Typing instruments have helped cement the "profile" of executives to the extent that to be something other than a combination of "extroverted thinker" and "introverted thinker" is career limiting. As far as cultivating the ability to think in human terms is concerned, many executives are developmentally challenged and, ironically, were selected to be where they are because of it. However, there are some who would do better in the HR arena if they had a safe and secure forum in which to discuss the significant issues they face, to lay the unvarnished truth out on the table for discussion, and to get some feedback. Professional associations are in the perfect position to provide the opportunity for this dialogue by offering forums for this purpose.

2. **Create linkages to related disciplines.** HR touches all parts of the organization and is therefore in a matrix position

with regard to engineering, finance, sales, marketing, and legal areas. The associations within the field need to bring in the influence of other associations and encourage activity of their members in other areas. For HR to become locked in to insular thinking as a discipline unto itself without connection to other major disciplines is a strategic blunder. Associations such as SHRM have the potential to be a source of integration as the expansion of the human network continues globally.

3. **Publish in other associations' periodicals.** Many associations are prone to giving sermons to the converted, but the nature of HR is pertinent to everyone, even when what is discussed amounts to commiseration or the sharing of common experience. The Project Management Institute and similar organizations often show that the largest problems they face in getting work done are related to their ability to deal with the human side of projects. Seminars such as those put on by the Institute for International Research (IIR) for the project management discipline have tracks for HR-related topics. However, HR conferences are not as effective when it comes to reaching into other worlds, such as that of project management, or having seasoned project managers speak directly to HR professionals about what they see their HR needs to be in the coming five to ten years. The same is true for periodicals. Most of the articles in publications for the HR community do not reach beyond the traditional HR domain. By publishing in places other than those inside HR, a more rich and diverse dialogue can be created that will integrate disciplines and make HR more of a central player on the team.

4. **Create an internship program.** People entering the HR ranks are in a slightly different risk profile than their technical counterparts. A software engineer can create prototype software and test it in an offline environment. An HR professional has to operate on live patients without the ability to model the effect of what is about to be done. Liability for a company that makes the wrong move from an HR perspective is immediate and

permanent. There is no such thing as bug fixing when people are involved. There is no way to undo a wrongful termination, for example. What would help would be for professional associations to create a globally recognized certificate program with teeth. One that involved the joint effort of educational institutions and businesses to create an internship program for people to serve in organizations under the coaching and mentorship of an HR coach to prepare them for the ever-changing needs of the real world.

How Higher Education Must Change

In addition to their training in general HR administration, today's HR professionals need to be educated in business management, organization development, change management, and organizational and individual psychology. For far too long, educational institutions involved in the preparation of HR professionals have mainly focused on preparing students in just the science of HR administration. This education involves a focus on state and federal legislation in areas of labor law, compensation, benefits administration, EEOC and affirmative action, and health and safety and training issues. However, effective HR management is a combination of both art and science, and the time and focused attention required to develop outstanding HR professionals have unfortunately been missing.

If institutions of higher learning are going to begin to meet the ever-changing needs of the business community, it is clear that the education and training of HR professionals will need to change. Students should be exposed much earlier—at the BA level—and in greater depth to such subjects as systems thinking, organizational behavior and psychology, and change management. There should also be distinct curricula for the HR specialist and the HR leadership. High-potential students should be identified early on and offered an "invitation to apply" to the newly formed HR leadership development program. This development program and its professors should be grounded in the realities of the business world in order for students to perfect both the science and the art of leading and organizing an HR department. In this way, a graduating student will not only have a BA degree but also carry the distinction of having begun the journey toward a future leadership role in HR.

HR leadership needs to be at the heart of any organizational transformation if the transformation is to be a truly sustained success. Transformation demands increasing speed and accuracy and the mastery of both the art and science of HR. We hope that in the wake of the economic downturn, organizations that have laid off hundreds if not thousands of graduate and postgraduate professionals will learn to place an even higher requirement on candidates who seek to join their organizations as they rebuild. Only by businesses demanding higher standards in hiring is the education system going to respond with an improved level of competency upon graduation.

Summary

During the twentieth century, when the acquisition of talent and the movement of people were largely based on the industrial model of thinking, HR developed accordingly. The industrial model of thinking became obsolete at least a decade ago, but somehow organizations have not completely responded to the change. The way in which HR organizations develop, are engaged in transformation, and brought in as a strategic partner in the organization is not the fault of any single aspect of the situation, but nevertheless needs significant attention to evolve to the next level of effectiveness. Leaders must acknowledge and act on the need to transform their HR organizations as an integral part of transforming the overall organization. HR organizations must engage proactively to improve their capabilities, competencies, and capacities to broaden the service provided to include organizational transformation needs and everything associated with them. Professional organizations must expand their definition of the role of HR professionals, working to encourage professional development of more diverse and in-depth business acumen. Go on those sales calls! The education system needs to add significant depth in business-related content to the requirements of people graduating with HR degrees. Ironically, HR, the organization that is a key player in transformation, also requires transformation. There is much to be done to make that happen. In the interim, organizations must take on the task of augmenting their HR capability if they hope to transform.

Ten Key Questions

1. Is your HR organization a strategic advantage?

2. Have you got the right people on the bus for transformation?

3. Have your strategy and transformation been translated into HR requirements?

4. Is your HR organization getting the basic job done? Does it have the capability to lead transformation?

5. Does your HR organization have the capacity to take on a more strategic role?

6. If you are in an academic role, have you begun to change the way HR professionals are educated?

7. If you are part of a professional association, have you begun to shift the conversation to be inclusive of organizational strategic planning, not just HR, and other related disciplines?

8. Has the organization taken on the challenge of putting A players in all key roles, starting at the top?

9. Do you develop HR professionals with rotational assignments so that they learn the business model?

10. How often has your HR organization been the driving force behind change?

7

YOUR CUSTOMERS ARE ALWAYS RIGHT, EXCEPT WHEN THEY AREN'T

Doing What Is Best for Customers Even When That Is Not Exactly What They Said They Wanted

> I know you thought you understood what I thought
> I said when I originally said what I wanted. But I am
> not sure you understand what I meant to say when I
> initially said what I had in mind. By the way, when
> will it be ready?
>
> —*Anonymous*

Southwest Airlines does its share of customer surveys to garner customer feedback. Other feedback comes from newspapers, the Internet, and federal ratings. A top complaint is the lack of assigned seats. One customer posted comments to *Online Travel Review* referring to the lack of assigned seats as a "miserable policy." In fact, being called "miserable" is one of the highest-frequency complaints Southwest receives. Still, the airline did not alter its boarding process until 2007, when it went from "conga lines," whereby people lined up on a first come, first served basis by A, B, and C groups, to "find your pole": people line up in five-person segments adjacent to poles with their boarding sequence number. For example, if someone has B43 on her boarding pass, she lines up with the second boarding group next to the pole that says 41–45 on its side. If this seems confusing, note that it confused customers for a period of time before eventual acceptance. People are still in A, B, and C groups, but under the find-your-pole scheme, the boarding is based on check-in time and not time spent in the boarding area. Southwest also extended its business model to allow for preferential boarding by selling the first fifteen slots in the first boarding group at a premium price.

So here we have a case of a company with an outstanding overall record of customer service and business performance that, despite some modifications to its seating assignments, does not permit customers to book a specific seat on their flights. Why? Because to do so would not fit with the overall system of Southwest service delivery. For instance, if people are on a flight that has two stops, they currently have the ability to change seats after the first segment. Allowing assigned seats would eliminate this flexibility. Second, anyone who has ever watched boarding gate behavior has noticed people attempting to upgrade and change seats, a process that causes a significant amount of gate-agent time and cost. The systems required to allow for assigned seating, the protocol for how to do it, the training to use the system, and so forth are not consistent with a low-cost, low-frill, point-to-point airline.

So, is the customer right in demanding preassigned seats? Of course customers should be able to express their dissatisfaction, but ultimately the answer is no, because what customers say they want will not allow for their more significant preference—low fares—which is why they fly Southwest in the first place. Saying no takes courage and resolve on the part of Southwest. Only by knowing its own business model can the company say no to customer demand in order to satisfy the greater need of the customer. Although the lack of assigned seating is likely to remain the number one complaint for Southwest, it is also one reason why Southwest's business model still works.

Although a products company may perform market research, product development, product prototyping, and so on based on feedback, very few products companies ever refuse to sell you their product because they don't think it's the right product for you.

If a person goes in to Wal-Mart and selects an over-the-counter medication that is not good for her, the person at the checkout counter will not refuse to sell it to her. The underlying logic is that it's up to the customer to know what is good for her. But this is not always the case. What customers can do is provide information as to what costs them time, makes their lives difficult, or impedes performance. And although customers are always right in asking for help with their problems, sometimes they don't know how to define their problems, so are not necessarily right in their assessment of what they need in order to solve those problems. They often have preconceived solutions in mind that are not in their best interest in either the short or long term. Further, your own salespeople will push you to offer exactly what their customers have said that they need to solve their problems. The question then becomes, What is driving action: the best solution or the fastest route to a commission?

Customers in Transformation

Providing what customers need and not what they ask for can function as the cornerstone for transformation (due to unique value propositions, blue oceans, loyal customers, and the motivational effect progress has on employees). Some companies develop a unique set of skills and abilities that think ahead of the marketplace, do the unconventional, and in some cases consciously choose not to do what the market asked for in order to offer what the market really needs. ALLDATA and APC are companies that did the background research, carefully thought through the alternatives, and did the unconventional in order to provide the exceptional. Similarly, Japanese car companies have historically offered less than what customers might want in terms of features in order to keep costs low. Although their tactics are different than APC's, for instance, the philosophy of doing what is best even though it goes against the explicit requests of customers is the same. All these companies serve as examples that can guide you in understanding what it means to uncover the implicit customer need, design a solution that's in the best interest of the customer, and deliver that solution in a cost-effective way.

ALLDATA—Taking the Road Less Traveled

When you take your car into an independent repair facility that handles multiple types and models of cars, do you think that the repair technician somehow magically knows how to fix all types of cars? Maybe you have never thought of it. Perhaps you don't really concern yourself with such things. All you want is to get the problem fixed. Behind the scenes, the technician needs to be able to find the problem and get information on how to fix the car so that he can tell you how much it will cost to do so. With thousands of cars and thousands of models, the shop technician must be able to access specific repair data among the millions of pages of repair manuals that exist.

In the auto industry, there are two principal types of car repair data. The first type is referred to as original equipment manufacturer (OEM) data, which come directly from the manufacturer and are harder for repair shops to access because they would have to have direct access to all car makers. The second, more easily accessed but less reliable data are reconstituted from the original OEM data. What the ALLDATA team did was consider what was best for the customer—OEM data—and figure out how to provide them directly, unaltered and unfiltered. Because ALLDATA was the first company to offer car repair information online, its customers didn't know the difference between OEM and reconstituted data. And had a market research team asked the potential customers which they wanted, they would not have had any way to answer because they didn't know the difference. Once the difference between OEM data and reconstituted data was made visible to the customer, ALLDATA became the leader in the field of repair data for automotive repair.

How Good Is Good Enough?

If you have purchased a battery backup system for your computer, did you analyze the basic power switching strategy that it is based on? If you have never made such a purchase, is this something that you would have on your shopping checklist? Like most people, you probably have no clue as to what backup battery systems are. But if you were asked whether you care about the most reliable and cost-effective way of protecting your computer and the data it holds, you might have an opinion and more interest in the question.

There are two principal ways of backing up power to your computer so that there is time to save your data in the event of a power loss. One way is to run the power through the battery, so to speak; if the building power is lost, the battery, or UPS, takes over. This gives the system time to save data and power off in a controlled manner. This is known as online UPS. The other way to approach the problem is to keep the battery in a parallel position and only engage the battery backup when power is lost. This is known as offline UPS, and it requires the UPS to switch very quickly when power is lost. Early APC customers asked for online UPS to protect their critical computers. Online was the prevailing UPS design among competitors at the time. In addition, the top vendors of UPS products were convinced that online units were required for critical applications like file servers, midrange computers, and critical engineering workstations. Customers were also trained to accept this wisdom.

APC studied the way computers used power and discovered that an offline design had some inherent advantages and was technically viable. One of APC's founders focused on this opportunity and was given the latitude to experiment with alternate designs. In the process, APC found that its new design was actually more efficient and more reliable over the long term. The offline design also provided cost advantages that translated to lower price points for the company's products. In order to cement its competitive position, APC enhanced its offer with unique software capabilities that improved the overall functionality of the total solution for customers. Software was offered free of charge and included with the purchase of the UPS. This combination of less expensive, more reliable, and software-enhanced products positioned APC for its fast journey to the top of the UPS market. In order to get the idea to market, APC focused on selling its new design to early adopters and used the demonstrated performance from this population to continue to expand its market share.

Should You Back Up the Backup?

If one is good, two is better. That is common logic. But what if two is not only worse but also more expensive? Double jeopardy. The customer pays more and gets less. What's wrong with this picture? Until APC disrupted it, the market had been convinced that full redundancy, meaning duplicate backup systems, both of which are capable of independently handling the demand, was the way to go. After all, redundancy of computer systems was the way we got a man to the moon; therefore it must be the best way to run a data center, right? Not exactly.

APC's larger products were used in critical corporate data centers and computer rooms. These data centers and computer rooms were critical to customers and supported the business processes of the enterprise, and the conventional wisdom was that a full redundant design was the way to go. These operations typically used two UPSs. If one failed, power would switch to the second backup unit. Most UPS vendors supported and marketed the model whereby they sold customers two UPSs with a switching device that automatically diverted power to the second UPS if the other one failed. But APC looked for another way. By applying some out-of-the-box thinking, the company actually came up with a way to give customers a redundant solution but with only one UPS. This meant customers did not need to buy a second UPS (a significant expense). APC developed a product with hot-swappable modules, whereby an extra module was included for redundancy that could be plugged in without shutting off the power. If one module failed, the rest of the system could support the computers while the bad module was swapped out for a new one.

APC extended its innovative thinking to the service side. Typically, larger UPS systems required power experts or electricians when service was required. Competing offers required power experts to come out and service the unit in the event of a failure, at additional cost and time delay to the customer. Because APC used a modular design, service was easy—virtually anyone could swap out a bad module. The overall result was full redundancy for customers at a much lower cost.

Customers are highly unlikely to ask for their power backup redundancy architecture to be redesigned. But few will turn down a significant cost reduction at a constant or improved risk profile. When the market is convinced of a way of doing things, only a supplier can think ahead of the market and find a disruptive way of adding value. It is not so much that customers are wrong; it is that they simply are blind to the opportunities.

Standardization Meets the Rack Mount

If you have ever visited a data center, you have seen what is known as a rack. It is a highly specialized storage unit that holds the servers and other computer equipment in stacks that are about twenty inches wide and six feet tall. Every data center is populated with them. As demand rose for different varieties of these racks, more companies started producing them, resulting in an explosion of equipment options and sourcing alternatives. APC entered the rack business to defend its UPS business when two of the large computer vendors tried to enter that market. In doing so, APC offered racks for mounting IT equipment for use in data centers, server rooms, and network closets.

The market was highly fragmented, but many large computer vendors, including IBM, HP, and Dell, marketed rack enclosures to their customers. The leading rack vendors offered catalogs full of racks and rack accessories for rack-mountable IT equipment. A typical vendor might offer tens of thousands of part numbers. These same vendors would often respond to custom product requests by customers. APC looked at its situation and endeavored to find a unique way to enter the market for racks and to position itself effectively versus its competitors. APC decided to break the model of offering many options for racks by offering only three different rack models. In doing so, they positioned themselves against the other suppliers by acting as a "neutral" offer that could accommodate all brands of leading rack-mounted IT equipment. Taking a page out of Henry Ford's book, APC offered racks in any color the customer wanted, as long as it was black. Through a limited standardized offering, APC was able to reduce costs and price, simplify the supply chain, increase availability around the world, and maximize quality. APC steadily gained market share year after year and became one of the top rack vendors in the world, despite a crowded field.

Was the customer right in the beginning to ask for customization of racks? In a sense, customers cannot be wrong for making a request. But in the long run, because the economy of standardization far outweighs the advantage of a unique design for things like rack mount hardware, treating a request for customization as gospel ultimately serves nobody. The issue here was that customers had no way and no incentive to collaborate on a standard platform, so they wouldn't consider that as an option. So when the customer population is collectively pushing for specialization, only the supplier can push standardization even though no customer asks for it. Although the customer may even oppose this approach, suppliers understand that standardization has delivered value to the market, even as computer interfaces have changed over time. APC applied this principle to its advantage and to the benefit of the customer.

InfraStruXure—a Study in Disruptive Behavior

What is the best way to compete in a field that is crowded and has a long-standing tradition of doing things one way? Change the rules of the game. Sounds simple until you try to do so. The chances of a customer demanding a change to the rules is close to zero. Thus fundamental change in the rules must come from the supplier, not the customer. In this case, customers can't know the answer because they don't understand the question.

Data centers were built the same way for decades, employing vendors, data center architects, consulting engineers, and a variety of contractors and other third parties. Each data center took months or even years to build due to its unique characteristics. Each was an expensive, unique "work of art." No two data centers were ever the same. This meant that the learning from the problems encountered building and operating one data center could never be directly applied to another. Most data centers were built for the future, with projected life cycles of ten years or longer. Each was built out with the maximum space, power, and cooling for the capacity it might need by the end of its lifetime. This meant data centers were always "overbuilt" for their needs today and required that customers build for the maximum capacity they might need in the future. Once built, data center demands under various conditions were unpredictable, and requirements and usage changed over time.

When it came to making a breakthrough in the way data centers are constructed, APC went about framing both the question and the answer. The company studied every aspect of data centers, from the way they were designed and constructed to the way they were managed and operated. The result was a unique integrated power and cooling architecture that changed the industry. APC created an overall architecture called InfraStruXure based on IT racks. It integrated power, cooling, and management features within these racks. The design allowed for a standardized, modular, scalable "pay as you grow" approach to building data centers. The unique APC software helped manage the overall offering. Hardware was offered in modules that could be easily swapped by nonexperts.

Customers never asked for InfraStruXure. They had lots of problems with building and operating data centers, but they typically only asked for small improvements in specific products or services. The InfraStruXure architecture reduced costs, simplified design, and improved performance. Competitors scrambled to copy it. InfraStruXure changed the data center industry. It was truly a disruptive innovation.

What Has Been Good for the Automobile May Be Good for You

Declaring that customers have a right to get their problems solved or their demands satisfied but not to dictate the method by which this happens is not a brand-new idea. The U.S. auto industry is a poster child for the combination of self-absorbed stale thinking combined with a lack of innovation. Starting in the 1960s and 1970s, while U.S. automakers remained entangled in their legacy and lethargy, the Japanese were busy figuring out how to think ahead of the market in terms of meeting implied customer needs and devising ways to incorporate insights into offerings.

Early car offerings were highly customized. It was not uncommon for customers to specify details, including the exact location of the headlights and steering wheel and other options. Early workers were called "fitters" because they custom-fit parts together. Eventually car companies standardized. In the extreme case, the Model T was offered with no options, and it came only in black. Later GM, Ford, and Chrysler offered many different models and many options. Although customers could not ask that their headlights be positioned just so, they had broad latitude in choices of exterior color, interior finish, and optional equipment.

This complexity in the overall car offers left customers with numerous and confusing options. It left car companies with inventory and supply chain challenges. Higher overall costs and complexity affected price and quality in a dramatic way. As cars got bigger, more expensive, and loaded with options, Toyota entered the market with small "good enough" cars with limited options. Initially quality was poor, but problems were fixed and reduced over time through Toyota's legendary Toyota Production System.

Customers had not directly asked for these small, inexpensive cars. But they had a real need, and Toyota filled it. After the oil crisis of the mid-1970s, Toyota was well positioned for strong growth and market penetration. Although some choices and complexity have been eliminated, many of the U.S. car companies still offer a myriad of models, color choices, and options to customers. The Japanese and many European car companies offer more limited choices. For instance, Honda offers a small number of cars, trucks, and SUVs through its Honda and Acura brands. Typically, these models have few or no options whatsoever. Furthermore, color choices are very limited. And if you pick a certain exterior color, the interior color and trim are fixed. You don't get to choose. This standardized approach had been a key ingredient to driving overall quality for Honda. It has simplified the selection process for customers. Despite not being able to pick every possible feature à la carte, Honda customers get high-quality cars at a great price.

The challenge is to think past the expressed need and look at the most optimized outcome for the customer and offer a solution at that optimization point. It may turn out that customers are not going to be happy about certain aspects, but they will be delighted overall because you focused on the composite picture of needs and not single aspects. Honda, Toyota, Subaru, and others have learned this lesson well.

What to Do to "Get It Right"

Organizations can take numerous actions to overcome some of their tendency toward insular thinking that prevents them from doing what is right for customers even when customers ask for something that is not in their best interest. The following sections offer what we have learned about the subject.

First, Go See the Customer!

When was the last time your executive staff went to directly observe the use of your products and services in their native environment (also known as your customer's location)? In some of the places we have worked over the years, there is little if any direct customer contact in the process of serving the customer. The result is that assumptions get made about customer needs, wants, and required outcomes without knowledge of the customer's real situation.

One automotive company philosophy states its criteria as "actual part, actual place, actual situation." What this means is that in order to understand the requirements for the part, you have to see the actual part in the actual place it is used and the actual situation in which it is used. This is exactly what we are advocating.

How adept is your organization at identifying how your customer actually experiences life? Many organizations remain insulated from the customer, to their detriment. To avoid this, you can

- Visit your customers at their places of business so you can see firsthand the issues they face.
- Observe a customer at work, listen to the customer describe his or her problems or challenges, and check to determine whether what you see matches what the customer is saying.
- Try to define the challenges your customers have in simple terms.
- Don't get trapped into automatically defining the solution before you really understand the problems and latent needs.
- Politely capture customer input, but don't assume customers know the solutions to their problems. Ask yourself at what level you are going to address their problems. Are you going to provide a product response, or are you looking to create a bundling of products and services to work on a more systemic

problem? Transformation changes the questions you ask and what you do with the information you gather.

- In short, constantly ask yourself, "If that is the answer, what was the question?"

Define the Customer's Problem Yourself

Customers are more attuned to symptoms than they are to causes. Which is more important in the long run, a bandage or the prevention of the injury? It is your job, as the supplier, to understand the difference between a symptom and a cause. After visiting a customer or a set of customers with certain challenges, use informal or formal techniques to define the problem.

Experience tells us that the process of defining what customers call a problem must go beyond expressed and unexpressed needs and beyond the recognition of latent need. What is required is to zoom in on the actual outcome that customers seek. Thinking beyond features and benefits yields better understanding of how to create differentiation. The most recent example of this is the focus on sustainability. One of the basic customer outcomes of purchasing a product that is environmentally sound is that the customer gets the sensation of getting what she wants from the product and at the same time feeling that she did something socially responsible. Like this one, almost all really compelling outcomes are emotional in nature.

Search for ideas that are "good enough" to solve the problem. For example, when customers struggled with the cost, complexity, and expertise required to run mainframe and minicomputers, the personal computer became good enough to run large businesses. Other good-enough solutions might come from applying technologies used in the home to commercial buildings or vice versa.

Look for different business models that exist in other industries that could be applied to yours and to your customers' challenges. Zipcar turned the traditional auto industry on its head by offering cars on a per-use basis much as software companies do. Particularly useful in big cities, Zipcar lets customers reserve a car for just the amount of time they need, and includes gas, insurance, and parking. Renting a Zipcar may not be the best of all possible solutions, but for many it is "good enough."

One approach to defining a customer need is to use the voice-of-customer (VOC) process. VOC is a market research process that captures customer requirements through feedback on their problems and needs. The output is used to drive decisions about product, process, or service requirements. If used correctly, VOC studies lead to innovative solutions to real customer problems. The process can use interviews, surveys, focus groups, observation, market data, quality data, customer service call data, and other sources. The output is then organized and prioritized in order of importance to the customer. The result should be an understanding of both the customers' stated and latent needs and critical input for new products, services, or processes.

As you attempt to define customer needs or problems, you will be constantly tempted to provide quick solutions driven by conventional thinking, or to tweak preexisting solutions that already exist on the market. Don't rush toward solutions. Be patient. Design your approach to the highest level of outcome you can identify. A low-level outcome merely stops the bleeding. A high-level outcome might have to do with system capability that reduces the risk of crashing, therefore eliminating the need for the bandage. Companies in transformation are moving up a ladder of inference in terms of the level of the solution they are providing. A bandage is a solution to an injury. Prevention is a solution to the system that brought about the injury. Companies in transformation must adjust their thinking to a higher level in terms of systems thinking related to customer outcomes.

Recognize Leading Signs of Opportunity

It has been said that any idiot can reduce his price. If that is the sole basis of competition for your organization, get ready for a long, low-performing slide into mediocrity. But perhaps instead we can all take a page from Bolthouse Farms' book. For over a century, Bolthouse has been in the farming industry, starting out in Michigan and now operating in several states, including California. The price of carrots is based on market dynamics. Supply and demand economics prevail. In order to grow and prosper, Bolthouse must find ways to increase efficiency and think outside the box in finding opportunities to extend its business model. Bolthouse has invested in research into how best to grow carrots, get them to market, and use process innovation to expand its production and product lines. It uses computer modeling to optimize irrigation and fertilization, which in turn optimizes yield and total production. In an old way of thinking, Bolthouse would simply have sought to expand acreage and find new markets for carrots. Instead, Bolthouse expanded into nutritional drinks and other products using the carrot juice derived from the processing of carrots as a base. Today, the company has eclipsed the sales of Odwalla juices with its brand of products that are an extension of its process and product innovation. Carrots are a commodity in every sense of the word until one considers the opportunity to innovate with regard to how they are grown, processed, packaged, and brought to market, and how the by-products of the process can be repurposed for everything from vegetable juice to cattle feed. Bolthouse Farms is a prime example of a company that has brought together innovative thinking, traditional values, technology implementation, and forward thinking.

For many organizations, the challenge is how to find the types of ideas that spark the kind of transformation that has occurred at Bolthouse Farms. There are three major signs of opportunity. One of the first indicators of an opportunity to do the unconventional is when someone says, "This is how it's done in this industry." If the computer industry stuck with the way things were done initially, we would have personal warehouses full of floppy disks, and large data centers would have acres of disk drives the size of large refrigerators.

The second major sign of opportunity is the existence of a standard that has been in place for a very long time. Perhaps stagnation has set in. This is an opportunity to move in and shake things up a bit. Furniture had been made for centuries in a similar fashion until companies began to sell it in kit form. Office furniture is large enough that a finished item cannot fit in a person's car, but the kit form with "some assembly required" will. The kit is the mechanism for people to be able to solve their need for a file cabinet without having to pay for delivery, which would add cost and time to the transaction.

The third major sign of opportunity relates to the possibility of rearranging a product, channel, service, or a combination of these. iTunes is an example of the rearrangement of the music distribution channel that eliminates physical creation of a medium in order to get music from artist to listener. iTunes did not invent music, nor did it invent music players themselves, but it did create a new way for an established product to reach the consumer globally, in infinite variety, with no inventory of physical merchandise. The ability to purchase one song at a time was also created in the process, which is enabled by the channel innovation.

Find Unique Solutions

Transformation is hard work. There is little point in changing an organization and ending up in a "me too" position. In laying out the overall transformation of a company, it is critical that the object of the transformation be designed to differentiate the organization, not merely to catch up to the competition. The risk is that you move forward only to find that the relative position you occupy is unchanged.

Find some way to add value that saves money, works faster, improves quality, or makes life easier for customers. Complexity is not our friend. Some of the most successful products (the iPhone, for instance) embed system complexity into a uniquely easy-to-use package. Conventional solutions are merely slightly improved versions of what's already on the market. They will eat up product management and engineering resources, and ultimately deliver slight or short-lived advantages for you versus your competitors.

Take time to **explore unusual alternatives.** Give engineers latitude to experiment and tinker before moving toward product definitions. Getting it right the first time is a myth. The truth is that success comes through lots of tries. Some are complete disasters. As Dave Kelley at IDEO says, "Fail often to succeed sooner."

Look for ways to **take waste out** of existing processes and currently accepted ways of doing things. Developing products that are easier to install, use, or service can save customers time and money, and make their lives easier.

Drive **standardized solutions** instead of offering customers every option. As we discussed earlier, the more successful car manufacturers do this very well. The result is fewer options for customers, but they have easier choices and higher quality in exchange.

Use **good enough** solutions. The best innovations come from the bottom up and replace more expensive solutions; they are not premium solutions that raise cost proportionately. In these situations, customers are "overserved" by the current solutions offered in the market. In the 1970s, Toyota introduced small, inexpensive good-enough cars for less. GM, Ford, and Chrysler ignored the threat. Today Toyota has overtaken the former number one car company.

Be different just because. Even though you want to drive real savings or improvements in performance, you simply can't compete long term if your products and services aren't differentiated from those of your competitors. When faced with two equal alternatives, pick the one that's different from the rest. Customers like new and different solutions. In general, innovation that drives customer satisfaction gives you long-term differentiation.

Unique solutions position you to move your company into blue oceans. A company that gets caught in the trap of offering only traditional solutions develops all sorts of problems. Teams get bored with making incremental improvements. Top talent eventually leaves. The company becomes exposed to possible extinction when competitors drive innovative solutions. When your company develops unique solutions and unique stories in the marketplace, it wins on many fronts. Employees are motivated and excited to work at the company. You attract new talent. Long-term sustainable competitive advantages ensure long-term prosperity. Innovation must be the norm. Innovation becomes a pillar for transformation and the generator of energy among the people in the organization. In the process, you create a fun place to work—which might be a transformation in and of itself.

Be Willing to Say No

The inability to say no is the beginning of a meltdown in your business. Every business has a core from which it originates and around which the business is built. The business is uniquely capable of doing some things well and other things poorly. Trying to do it all is a recipe for disaster. Added to this is the tendency for businesses to take on things that they know or suspect are bad for the customer; they cave in to revenue pressure or simple hubris and say yes when they should say no.

Fundamentally, the question becomes whether you are after popularity or respect. Say yes, and you will be popular. Say yes to the wrong thing, and you will be popular for a while until you lose that popularity to the reality of delivering the wrong thing. At that point, respect is lost too. The only way to gain both popularity and respect is to apply wisdom and courage to the process of selecting what you will and will not stand for. Note that customers may initially be mad at you for going off and producing something they did not directly ask for. That's OK! Your sales force may also be angry. Channel partners may be angry. That's OK too! Eventually they will be happy that you took the time to give them the innovative solutions that meet their customers' real needs and make it easy to sell against the competition. Get up the nerve to say no to customers when they tell you exactly what they need to solve their problems, when you know that what they are asking for is not in their best interest. Don't create a back door. Customers will often take what you are offering if you don't also offer them exactly what they asked for. Avoid letting sales dictate product road maps or define product needs. Sticking with products and services because they are easy to sell may not be the most sustainable way to reach your goals. Say no to easy but ineffective solutions too!

Transformation Changes What Is "Right"

In a pure products company, what optimizes a customer's experience is product features and benefits as they relate to the direct use of the product. To use ALLDATA as an example, its product called Repair is designed as a subscription service for automobile repair shops to access OEM information as to how to repair an automobile. What "right" means in this case is the best available information, accessible 24/7 for all makes and models of cars built after a certain date. The systemic inference is that the better the information, the better the estimate, the more efficient and effective the repair, the better customers are served, the better the reputation of the shop for quality work. ALLDATA excels at delivering the best information available. The company has no equal in Repair. Now let's take a look at the product called Manage. Manage is a software program that handles several aspects of managing a repair shop. Customer data, estimating, scheduling, repair order creation, and repair information such as time and parts cost per repair are all included. It allows a company to automate the generation and processing of repair orders. It also hooks up to accounting software for generating reports. Whereas Repair optimizes repair efficiency, Manage is designed to optimize shop performance. A business model that was created to optimize repair efficiency is not the same as one designed to optimize shop performance. When a company makes a fundamental change in what it is optimizing for a customer, the subject of what there is to be "right" about fundamentally changes. In the case of ALL-DATA, a large portion of the customer population is focused not on optimizing shop performance but on optimizing repair efficiency. Therefore, there is much work to do to position products such as Manage in the marketplace and prepare the ALLDATA organization to meet the challenge of a different kind of "right." All the lessons in this chapter must be viewed in relation to this fundamental concept: when there is a change in the definition of what there is to be "right" about, transformation is in play. In many businesses, this is the difference between a historical focus on products and a new focus on bundled solutions. It sounds so easy when it rolls out of the strategic planning process. When transformation hits the reality of the customer interface, things get a little more interesting.

Summary

Customers are always right in asking for help with their problems. Our experience tells us that customers are less adept at providing insightful solutions. The reason is simple: customers experience a single data point in space; they have no way to do pattern analysis or latent needs analysis of a marketplace. Only you can do that as an observer of the overall picture.

When businesses take the path of expedience, delivering a shortsighted solution, they do themselves and the market a disservice in the long run. Just as auto companies did a disservice to the marketplace and themselves by creating too many brands with too many options, you also can create long-term damage by not taking a broader view. Overreacting to a small set of inputs from customers may put your resources to work on a solution that is far from your best course of action. You are probably far better off if you design your actions by understanding the latent need of your customers and gain as much of your knowledge as possible through direct contact with them. In the process, you are going to get asked to do some things that are either outside your capability or outside your ethics. In both cases, you need to learn to say no. This takes discipline and is a mini-transformation in itself.

In the transformation of your business, the relationship you have with customers may need to change dramatically. The questions you ask as a pure products producer are going to differ greatly from those you ask as a solutions organization. Changing the focus from product features and benefits to the solution perspective of optimized systems is a large leap for companies. The type and nature of the inquiry into customer problems change as you consider more complex systems issues. The customer is in no position to take a marketwide view of opportunities as a solution organization, so the responsibility rests with your company to take on the challenge of being a trusted adviser. Sometimes trusted advisers are unpopular, as their advice conflicts with customers' preconceived notions. The advice also might create unrest within part of the customers' organizations that must change as a result of what you have to say. The industry that represents the old way of doing business will likely rise up to discredit your new approach, so be ready for lots of push-back from multiple sources. Remember, anyone who does well in a system—even when it becomes obsolete—defends that system. Old ideas and old habits die hard. The best way to arm yourself with the best information is through direct observation of customer challenges. When your customers and competitors and some of your own staff begin the inevitable counterargument, you can rely on the fact that one good piece of data outweighs a thousand expert opinions. In the end, the customer will thank you, your people will be better off, and your competitors will not know what hit them.

The acid test of transformation relative to doing the unconventional is whether you are prepared to bet the farm. Most companies that have made it big have been able to place a big bet and bet the future of the company. IBM did so with System 360; Cisco did with Voice over Internet Protocol. The question is whether your organization believes enough in the direction you are headed to place the big bet.

Ten Key Questions

1. Does your company support the old adage that the customer is always right, even when there is evidence to the contrary?

2. When customers ask for a specific product or service, do you simply provide it?

3. When was the last time you said no to a customer?

4. How are your solutions unique in comparison with those of your competitors?

5. When was the last time you examined the myths that exist in your industry?

6. How long has the status quo been in effect in your business?

7. Are you willing to place a big bet on an innovation?

8. How many unique and differentiated moves do you have in your development pipeline?

9. How does transformation change the definition of what is "right" in your company?

10. Do people in your organization have the latitude to explore solutions that are unconventional?

8

DON'T LET ANALYSTS RUN YOUR BUSINESS

Those Aren't Their Assets on the Line—They're Yours!

> Tell you what ... you go start my car; I will stay
> here and honk your horn for you.
> —*Motorist with a stalled car on the freeway*

When a behind-the-scenes critic, commentator, or analyst is right, he can claim to be brilliant. When wrong, he claims it is someone else's fault. He has an advantage over the companies he studies. When a company announces earnings and they exceed expectations, it is a good day for the stock. When earnings do not meet expectations, it is a bad day for the stock. Whereas the analyst's prediction does not alter the reality of the situation, the value of a company goes up or down based on the difference between the prediction and the actual outcome. In other words, the person with the most power (the analyst) has the least stake in the outcome and the least accountability. Analysts make no decisions, provide no information to the system, have no accountability for being dead wrong—yet they still heavily influence the behavior of the market.

An Example Relationship

In the process of growing GenCo, there were numerous occasions when the market analysts were less than pleased with the answers GenCo provided. At the end of the day, however, it is the leadership team who sets the strategic direction for the company and is ultimately responsible for company performance. The leadership team at GenCo often took the less obvious, higher-risk course of action that generated significant value for the enterprise. The pivotal decisions GenCo made along the way about what to do and why to do it, how those decisions conflicted with analysts' opinions, what value GenCo created—all provide a significant learning opportunity. GenCo showed courage in setting aside short-term popularity for long-term respect. GenCo's going against conventional wisdom to justify its decisions provides a great example for executives facing an increasing amount of uncertainty in the environment of today's global enterprise.

Early GenCo

In the beginning, GenCo produced commercial building products. Not long after forming the company, the founders could see that the market was not a viable business at a time when GenCo had limited private capital. The founders soon elected to shift their entire focus onto the products that attach to computers. Because there was private funding, the management team at GenCo did not have to spend any time convincing a large group of people that this was a viable move. In addition, the leadership team at GenCo allowed only a limited amount of venture capital so that the venture capital community would not own a controlling interest in the company. Further, rather than seeking additional funding, GenCo chose to fund their growth with their own money, which further reduced the amount of explanation required.

After gaining momentum in the computer market, GenCo chose to go public, and became a small cap NASDAQ stock. GenCo's strong cash position and profit levels kept the attention of stock analysts and earned their praise. As the company grew, GenCo hired a large number of very young people whose preference for lower salaries in return for more stock options created a culture of extremely frugal people motivated primarily by business performance.

Most analysts liked GenCo's business performance but were less sure about its strategy and business model. With less expensive architecture, GenCo could distribute its products in volume through PC equipment suppliers and catalogs rather than through high-end value-added resellers (VARs). Analysts were skeptical about GenCo's use of high-volume channels, but with continued strong company performance, stock analysts continued to cautiously support GenCo. The company's strong performance also affected GenCo's internal support system, leading employees to exhibit "ownership behavior": as the stock price rose, the value of employee stock grew, which in turn resulted in better business decisions being made by employees, driven by their own self-interest.

GENCO Learns to Manage the Analysts

Contrary to most publicly traded companies, GenCo decided that it would not engage in the earnings-versus-projection game that makes up a large part of an analyst's job. The analyst community was less than pleased, because estimating earnings projections is part of what analysts do for a living. However, GenCo didn't see the value in it and therefore elected not to play. In addition, GenCo released highly scripted—and highly similar—earnings announcements and investor calls. The head of investor relations, the CFO, and the CEO all read from the same script. Both of these were gutsy moves by GenCo.

As GenCo began its transformation into the large systems business, it also adopted one other major communication strategy with analysts. After purchasing a Danish company called CordCo in 1999, GenCo minimized the amount of information provided to analysts about the acquisition and its subsequent strategic impact on GenCo. Although this kept the nature of the acquisition strategy private to the leadership team in GenCo, it also served to frustrate the analyst community. This strategy came back to haunt the company. With the Y2K wave and the dot-com boom and bust, GenCo continued to make significant investments without a lot of explanation. This meant that in a time of economic downturn, GenCo was making significant additional investments while others were cutting back, which made analysts nervous. With a lack of transparency and an unconventional investment strategy, there was a strain on GenCo's relationship with the analyst community.

Getting into large systems, shifting from transactional to relational models, and educating the market on a new way to create solutions all require investments that hurt short-term results. In addition, GenCo had to figure out a way to build its enterprise sales force so that it could handle transactional sales of volume products. This entails a significant investment in people, systems, and training. And while the company was out recruiting and training new partners, conducting educational events on a massive scale, and spending significant amounts on R&D, analysts were very frustrated at the lack of understanding.

In the end, these investments culminated in GenCo's successfully disrupting the market in large systems and emerging as the clear leader in their field. Sales of the large systems business grew strongly. In fact, GenCo's results were so strong that a larger company elected to acquire GenCo, which added significant value to the acquiring company. In the end, GenCo underwent transformation three times: once when it went from producing commercial products to producing computer products; again when it moved to large systems; and yet again when it was acquired.

Putting the Idea to Work

The real value in any example is being able to translate the example into action for your benefit. The following sections contain suggestions on how you may be able to implement a strategy for successfully interfacing with the analyst community.

Run the Business as If It Were Your Own

If your company was yours and yours alone, you wouldn't make decisions just to make a certain profit in a certain quarter. So don't do it for Wall Street. Take a look at the decisions you make to drive long-term value and ask yourself if you are shortchanging investments simply to make your quarterly earnings look better. In periods of growth as well as in an economic downturn, making a cut in critical spending simply to diminish a negative quarterly result will cause long-term harm to both the company's development and to its critical skill base. Knowing that shareholders will ultimately thank you may be the only solace in making a decision that is unpopular with analysts but critical to the business.

People learn to spend money as if it were their own by being treated like owners. It is necessary to move from a perspective of "Who cares? It's not my money" to one where people feel a sense of personal discomfort every time a dime is wasted. You know that employees have this sense of ownership when you hear them mention that a plane ticket, meal, or hotel was too expensive—or that a particular initiative inside the company was wasteful. You can also hear the common response: "Why would you worry about it? It's not your company [or your money]," which indicates the difference in a feeling of ownership. If people are analyzing spending on a plane ticket and making good decisions, the analysts at the top of the business are going to see the cost control results.

The easiest way to make people feel like owners is to give them stock or stock options in the company, or to allow them to buy in with their own money. One of us worked for a dot-com called Mariner One, where he was expected to invest his own money, rarely get paid, and only occasionally have travel expenses reimbursed. This is an extreme scenario, but it does serve as a clear example of ownership. Another way to instill a sense of ownership is to delegate responsibility so that people will feel as if they own overall portions of the business. It also works to reward people who act in the best financial interests of the company without necessarily getting paid for it in terms of formal and informal recognition, raises, bonuses, or even promotions. The idea is to create a culture where people care about, comment on, and responsibly manage expenditures, and where acting outside this cultural norm means facing criticism or even rejection.

The culture at GenCo was very effective in determining the critical level of spending. Historically GenCo acted frugally with respect to travel expenses, office space, and perks, while never skimping on R&D. The company searched for alternative formulas in sales and marketing that relied on an inexpensive scalable type of spending (marketing and channel partners) rather than salespeople, who could be expensive. In fact, GenCo shaped its portfolio management, by pursuing as many push-the-leading-edge projects as it could manage within its limited resources. It did benchmark R&D, open models, gross margin structures, and revenue growth against its key competitors, but this was more of an afterthought. GenCo was absolutely mindful of the limits on it as a public company, which also served to limit what was an acceptable expense level.

Focus on the Long Term

Focusing on the long term is extremely beneficial—if you know what the long term is. Many organizations don't give much thought to targets and goals that reach out three or more years. In "Whatever Happened to Silicon Valley Innovation?" (*BusinessWeek*, Dec. 31, 2008), Steve Hamm revealed that Silicon Valley is beginning to show serious signs of a lack of innovation. Most advances in organizations that are famous for breakthrough innovation are becoming incremental and lackluster. Without a redistribution of investment into leading-edge innovation, Silicon Valley is likely to decline as a significant contributor to the national economy.

Only time will tell. What is obvious now is that there has been a significant change in the investment pattern in fundamental research and innovation. Look at your own organization. How much investment is being made in long-term projects and programs? When you have had cutbacks, how many long-term innovation projects have been diminished or removed? Companies who make high-quality decisions consider the long-range implications of making an investment or disinvestment. Companies cannot declare a transformation in progress and then derail efforts due to a quarterly earnings deviation from "analysts' expectations" if they hope to be successful.

Before making significant cutbacks, create a vision of where you want to go, and undertake projects that will have lasting impact and long-term competitive advantage. Invest intelligently in key projects, initiatives, and assets that will deliver a winning formula over the long term. When analysts criticize you or downgrade your stock, or when the stock market punishes you for recent results, put your head down and do the right thing for the long term. You will only delay your pain if you try to make quick fixes to problems.

Divest from Businesses or Product Lines That Don't Match Your Vision

As one CEO put it, "I know that division costs a lot of money and it loses money every year, but I just feel like I 'should' have it." It can be very difficult to give up parts of your business that have been a key element of your success. Analysts may criticize you for exiting profitable businesses that still contribute positively to the bottom line but that you know don't fit your future business. You will also experience substantial internal resistance to exiting businesses to which people have become attached. But remember that the analyst community does not have a problem with inorganic growth through merger and acquisition, even when the merger is ill-advised. They are also not well equipped to deal with inorganic shrinkage, even when the bottom line would benefit from the company's getting rid of a poor-fitting, underperforming portion of the business. In one case, a CEO and his team failed to discontinue a line of products that was far from profitable, stating the need to maintain "top line revenue" for appearance purposes. Such thinking reveals a fear of making hard decisions that may veer from analysts' recommendations. In the end, postponing important decisions about selling off business units that do not fit the future of the company is a drain on brain capacity in the executive suite and will bring your transformation to a standstill. Specifically consider some or all of the following:

- With the future identity of your company in mind, map out the businesses and product lines that should make up the core of your offering.
- Identify businesses and product lines that don't make sense in your new vision for your company.
- Develop plans to exit these businesses as soon as possible. There are many options here, including simple shutdown of a division, sale of a portion of your business, repositioning or rebranding of product lines, and licensing out rights to certain products.
- Extensively communicate with employees affected by changes in your offer, during what can be an emotional period.
- Execute exit plans swiftly. It's better to rip a bandage off quickly than to pull it slowly across the skin.

Don't Change Course Just Because Analysts Can't See Where You're Going

One company we know began to look at the relative performance of various parts of its business in the midst of its transformation. One drastically underperforming portion of the business was not central to its core business, begging the question of how the company got into that business in the first place. The answer was that the company had been able to get the acquisition approved. There was no discussion about strategic fit. The lesson here? Taking actions in business based on what you can get approval for as opposed to what will create the best results in the long term is a dangerous practice.

It is true that some organizational strategies are hard to understand without in-depth knowledge of the business model and all its nuances. Some levels of innovation are impossible to prove beyond a shadow of a doubt. The more innovative the direction you are taking, the more difficult it is to prove. There was little proof for the founding of Google, Yahoo, Facebook, or YouTube, or the launching of the personal computer or the office copier. If you're taking an unexpected business direction, analysts may not understand why you are going that way, and you may have a tough time convincing them that your chosen course is the best one. You can't expect analysts to take everything on faith, but you also should not stop transformation simply because they don't have any. Realize that your business may have some secret sauce that just can't be explained—or you may not want to share the recipe. There may be a prevailing view from the market, analysts, and competitors that you're going the wrong way or that you're doing something that "just isn't done" in your industry. This is a very good sign! But it may take a long time for analysts to see the magic in the method to your madness.

Invest During Downturns to Get Ready When the Sun Comes Out

The economic downturn of 2007, 2008, and 2009 has brought about a huge challenge for most businesses. Although catastrophic in many ways, the economic collapse also provides an unprecedented opportunity. Because of the rollback in prices, hard assets have never been cheaper. And if there is ever a time to retool the skill base of a company, it is when there is a surplus of talent available in the marketplace due to layoffs. In addition, the economic downturn creates a need and urgency for organizational change, which is very difficult to create in good times yet is necessary for transformation.

During these times, careful response to opportunities can be the source of significant growth moving forward. If an organization needs to make a cutback of approximately 10 percent in order to achieve a modified set of goals, it should consider making a 20 percent cut. If an organization merely cuts back the minimum amount it has to in order to achieve targets, chances are that any slack that can be devoted to innovation in transformation is going to be cut with it. Therefore, companies should consider making expense reductions in order to create some slack and the discretionary spending capability to bring about fundamental changes. In making such a move, the company can make sure that a portion of R&D goes toward tinkering, experimenting, or other high-risk, high-return ventures. Companies can also benefit if they seek out competitors' top talent—especially R&D talent, sales talent, and management or generalist leaders—who may be exiting an undesirable work environment. Companies can also use this time to solidify customer relationships through focus on existing customers and their needs, including service contracts, upgrades, planning for future opportunities, and other support.

Create Owners with Stock—Make Your Own Internal Analysts

To garner support from top management and key employees, make substantial stock or stock option grants on an ongoing basis. This may be the single most powerful thing a company can do. Employees with stock options that constitute a substantial percentage of their income act like owners because they *are* owners. They can also be helpful internal analysts because they have the in-depth knowledge to make significant recommendations and because it is in their best interest to suggest strategies that work in the short and long terms. We've seen key employees make the right decisions for the long-term health of the business, even when it directly and negatively affects their own short-term bonus compensation. The potential dilution of their stock options or restricted share grants is more than made up for by a critical mass of employees motivated to drive long-term success for the company. What Wall Street analyst wouldn't want that?

Create Turnkey Presentations

Anyone who has played the telephone game in which a message is passed from person to person understands how communication gets spun with every new person in the system. After being transmitted through about five people, the original message is virtually unrecognizable. Transformation is much like that original message. But unlike the message in the telephone game, the communication of transformation cannot be passed informally from person to person. Transformation requires a simple, repeatable, consistent message to permeate the organization, which means working with the communications department to develop careful messaging to explain current results and your long-term vision and strategy. Specifically, consider the following approaches.

Train Your Management Team to "Stick to the Script." There is a time for creativity and a time for uniformity. Get very creative in the development of the script. Once the script is written, don't allow the show to be turned into an "improv" where each leader creates his or her very own slide deck and spin on the message. People in corporate branding protect the consistency and precision with which corporate logos are printed, displayed, and reproduced. Most corporate branding people are brutal in defense of standardization of how a logo is used. The same approach is needed with regard to messaging in the company. Anyone who is off-message needs to be corrected as a first order of business because confusion of the message is catastrophic.

Make Sure Everyone Is Aligned. By aligned, we mean that people have had an opportunity to participate, interject, push back, argue, criticize, and contribute and are in basic support of the direction and speed of the company. At the end of all the wrestling over what the message is, people have to meet the minimum level of buy-in. Here is how we define *consensus:* "Consensus means you can live with it." Not that you are necessarily pleased or pumped up about it. But at least you can live with it and support making the decision successful. Anyone who is demonstrating that he or she is not at the minimum level of buy-in needs coaching to get on the bus or needs to be shown the station exit.

Practice, Practice, Practice for Presentations with Wall Street. Winging it is not a great strategy for outbound communication. Take the time for multiple practice sessions before every communication. This means really listening to the presentation. It means putting down the smart phones and PDAs long enough to pay attention and give constructive feedback on the messaging and delivery. This feedback would include coaching on tone, energy, pace, level of detail, and completeness.

Use Scripted Communications in Earnings Calls and Presentations. This may be awkward at first, but analysts will become accustomed to this approach and adapt. Develop a set of standard reporting categories and formats. Stick to it. Add information only when there is a clear justification. Information is like rope. Given enough, we can all get ourselves tangled up in it or worse.

Avoid Vague Strategy and Mission Statements That Aren't Meaningful. The world is full of smart-talk-based presentations that use terminology such as *disruptive innovation, ambidexterity, game changing, next generation, version 2.0,* and other smart-sounding phrases to describe where the company is going. Keep it simple, straightforward, and nonsense free.

Offer Practical Examples to Illustrate Your Strategy. In its advertising, Apple has begun to show examples of how the iPhone is used. The ads are simple and straightforward, and they highlight the practical use of new applications as well as how to use basic functionality on the device. If your strategy is to develop renewable energy products, talk about how the products are used in practical terms, by whom, and to what benefit. Avoid delving into technology discussions that would be interesting to a subatomic physicist but will bore the hell out of an analyst.

Manage Your Investor Base

Being publicly traded is at least a two-edged sword. One edge is investor capital, the blood that sustains the organization's functions. With capital comes investors, however, which is the other edge of the sword. Investor relationships are critically important, but can be problematic. It is critical to make communication decisions carefully in order to determine the maintenance cost of dealing with the investment community. It is a good idea to develop a competent investor relations team that can effectively manage the investor base. This is a highly specialized field and requires dedicated resources, but if such management is done correctly, the cost will be more than offset by fewer investor-related issues. Executives need to focus on creating results. A dedicated investor relations team can be a great investment in increasing executive capacity.

It is also important to build a diversified investor base. You want to make sure you have one or two large institutional investors, but seek out the ones you want. Diversification is critical in terms of both outside interference and the impact of an investor leaving the stock.

Meet with analysts regularly and expand the interface with analysts beyond the CEO, CFO, and head of investor relations to include business unit leaders, directors, and VPs. This will create two principal effects. First, it will show the analysts that you have organizational bench strength. Second, it will drive a deeper level of commitment in the organization: there is nothing like having the responsibility to present information to increase the ownership of the information. In addition, it is helpful to hold effective and professional annual shareholder meetings, but keep the venue, amenities, and agenda tailored to the investors you wish to engage. It will keep some of the undesirable people out of the punch bowl.

Build an Effective but Externally Impressive Board of Directors

The board of a company is an internal consultancy that can be relied on to provide guidance. Analysts look at the makeup of boards and either gain or lose confidence according to who they see is backing the organization. In thinking about whom to hire, consider that the purpose of the board is to deliver the business guidance you need most. Boards should be made up of people who fit the strategic agenda, and they should be replaced as the agenda evolves. It also helps to have well-known, recognized, highly regarded leaders from industry or the public sector on your board. Information coming from a recognized leader is given more credibility than it would if it were coming from a relative unknown. If you have widely recognized and respected players on the board, the job of working with analysts is much easier. And no one is on the board for life. As we noted here, board members need to come and go. Just because you added them does not mean you have to treat them like Supreme Court justices. We all have our strengths and weaknesses. When the weaknesses outweigh the strengths, it is time to make a change.

Board members should be able to work together as an effective team, while still being diverse enough that multiple perspectives are always considered. This can be a tricky balance. You don't want the board always to agree, but you also don't want board meetings to end up in feuds and fights. The board must be able to handle healthy conflict successfully.

Have an odd number of board members! Some decisions in transformation are tough, ambiguous, and divisive. Perhaps you will have a lot of five-four splits in the voting, but with an odd number you at least have a resolution path, whereas with an even number, you may not.

Give Analysts Something to Work With

Analysts have a job to accomplish. They get paid to take a look at projected performance and provide guidance to the market. It will create greater value for the analysts and you if you focus on providing information that is useful to them and of the type that you should have readily available anyway. Communicating effectively with analysts means being able to describe an inspiring vision, a strategy, and high-level goals at any time, analyst meetings included. The nature of transformation includes the articulation of how these attributes are changing, so the material should be close at hand. Do this enough, and you may get a pass from the analysts as you transform. Also make it a habit to undercommit and overdeliver. Do not overcommit on expectations, but do not give sandbag estimates either. The key is to generate credibility by delivering on the expectations you set. Or you can consider not giving revenue or earnings estimates at all! This will cause some heartburn for the analysts, but you are probably better off taking the heat for not giving guidance than you are in playing the estimation game. By definition, an estimate has a 50-50 chance of being over or under a given value. Those are not great odds where the gain in value for exceeding estimates is not as large as the loss from not reaching the projection. You're better off staying out of the game. Remember that Las Vegas was built on money taken from people who came up on the wrong side of the odds.

Be frugal where it won't hurt your long-term business. Avoid expensive company events, first-class travel and entertainment, fancy office buildings, and unnecessary perks for employees. Analysts will take notice, and you won't have to make the wrong business decisions just to please them for the short term.

It is amazing that people advertise that they have cut back on unnecessary spending as recession hits and layoffs are in progress. It makes more sense not to overspend at any point under any circumstances. Think of the advantages of announcing no change in spending as a result of a downturn, being able simply to continue with the same frugal pattern. Think of the time and business controls hassle that might be avoided as a result.

Last, show you can listen to the feedback you get from analysts. Step back from your own views every now and then to gain perspective. Analysts may just save you from yourself once in a while. We all get very close to our organizations, and we see lots of trees. However, the view of the forest is critical also. It is possible that the analysts could add some value in providing a viewpoint that has not been considered. When this is the case, show them that you heard them by responding to their input. It could go a long way toward solidifying the relationship.

Summary

Transforming the business is the only way many businesses will drive long-term success. Rare are the business models such as those of Southwest Airlines and Wal-Mart that are decades old and still thriving. At the same time, providing return on investor capital is critical, even though the business model must evolve or fade into irrelevance. Ultimately, analysts should be pleased with the results, but they won't be happy along the way. Giving in to the short-term pressure exerted by analysts is counterstrategic to transformation. In many cases, the analysts simply won't understand your transformation strategy, and your spending a disproportionate amount of time trying to explain it is a waste of enterprise resources. Better to spend your time

- Thinking long term and designing strategy such that everybody wins
- Avoiding the lure of short-term results that placate analysts

- Using stock incentives aggressively
- Developing your people to be internal analysts
- Standardizing your approach to outside communication
- Using your bench strength to develop communications and build analyst relationships
- Communicating with analysts on what you're doing and why you'll win

Ten Key Questions

1. Do you find yourself designing your business with the analyst in mind?

2. Does the statement "What the &*!%# are we going to tell the analysts?" come up in conversations often?

3. How many shareholders are also employees?

4. Do you use stock incentives? How deep and wide are your programs?

5. How often do you meet with analysts individually or in small groups to explain your strategy and vision?

6. Is it always the same team of people that meet with the analysts, or do you spread the responsibility?

7. Do you trust people in the organization to handle an analyst meeting?

8. Do you limit what is said outside the company?

9. Do you script your communications for uniformity?

10. To what degree does the organization listen to analysts?

9

MERGER IS NOT
A FOUR-LETTER WORD

Things that matter most must never be at the mercy
of things that matter least.
The first sign we don't know what we are doing is
an obsession with numbers.
—*Johann Wolfgang von Goethe*

On a typical day in mergers and acquisitions, the headlines and
articles might include the following: a small utility company
acquires a portion of a large company that is larger than it is.
In the process of the little fish eating the big fish, the acquiring
company realizes that it has not only acquired a new business but
is the proud owner of relationships with five very strong unions
that it doesn't know how to deal with and a marketplace it does
not understand. In another part of the world, a large conglomerate
business buys a company one-third its size and merges it with
an existing business unit. The existing business unit is one-third
the size of the acquired unit. The smaller unit is part of the
long-standing structure of the acquiring company. Under these
circumstances, who acquired whom? Whom is the merger with,
exactly? In yet another corner of the world, a telecom company
merges with a larger company. The merger triples its revenue,
but detracts from its bottom line and increases its business model
complexity. And the beat goes on.

The word *merger* has six letters, but it conjures up four-letter
words for many executives. In some ways, mergers are the
things many people love to hate. Although there seems to be

a never-ending stream of brilliant matches made in heaven between strategic alliances and, in some cases, major misfits, the results of mergers and acquisitions (M&As) are almost uniformly dismal. Much has been studied and written about the efficacy of growth through M&A. Most estimates put the success rate at between 30 and 40 percent. Yet the pace of M&As does not seem to be slowing down.

So given that M&As are often chosen as growth strategies, what can be done? If the chances of success in a given merger are about three out of ten, how can an organization increase its chances of being among the three? We have worked in and around M&As made by Monsanto, APC, Schneider Electric, IBM, and numerous smaller businesses. We have noticed significant opportunities for improvement in how to diagnose and execute a merger in ways that promote the health and well-being of the organization and the people in the system. Further, we have seen that the effect of mergers is largely predictable. From these experiences, we have compiled a few lessons (described later in the chapter) to help address issues we have faced and provide guidance where possible.

Rather than focusing on operational efficiencies, or synergies as they are sometimes called, we advise starting at the roots of each organization. By examining the patterns of development in each organization and setting them next to each other for comparison and for action, we can help diagnose significant M&A issues. In many mergers, there is a tendency to focus on a limited number of things, such as product development road maps and the lowering of back-office costs. There is often less emphasis placed on talent retention, organizational redesign, impact to people and communities, environmental impact, and integration of corporate DNA. We operate on the assumption that a significant portion of the value being acquired in a merger is in the people of the acquisition. If the merger or acquisition is for technology, process, channels, or other tangible assets—in other words, if the people of the acquired entity are of little to no value to the acquiring entity—this chapter is of no value. On the basis of our experience, our recommendations are grounded in the assumption that people are at the center of the value equation in both parts of the merger. Merger planning and execution must go beyond synergies and reach into the arena of sustainability. By sustainability, we mean the combination of financial, ecological, and sociological sustainability. Today's enterprise must focus on the money, the environment, and the people. The opportunity here is to create a merger that will last and that will yield a stronger enterprise.

Some mergers look good on paper but end up degrading performance and therefore value. As an example, the following is an excerpt from a Gartner analysis of tool sets in the project portfolio management arena that are offered by HP, Microsoft, and others ("HP PPM," http://mediaproducts.gartner.com/reprints/ca/157924.html). The context of this example is the acquisition of Mercury by Hewlett-Packard. First is the assessment of the technical aspects of HP's portfolio management tool set:

Strengths

- Multiple request types, from demand to closure, are analyzed readily and can be offered in dashboards that are filterable by users who can create (and distribute) dashboards/portlets.

- HP has been realizing an ITPC vision, with the PPM Center positioned alongside the Quality Center and HP Service Management Center.

- HP can offer its PPM Center in broader deals to leverage relationships and provide discounts to customers in the broad HP software installed base.

Roughly translated, this means

- Features and functions are in great shape.
- Product integration is looking good.
- The product from the acquisition can be integrated into a larger offer that delivers benefits for the customer in terms of the comprehensiveness of the offer and the overall cost.

So far so good in terms of product features and functions and the like, but read on as to what Gartner has to say relative to the nontechnical aspects of the acquisition:

Cautions

- Under the ownership of HP (since its acquisition of Mercury), PPM product development has slowed, because management has shifted, and the point release targeted for 2007 is now slated for second-quarter 2008.
- Customers cite improved support following a drop-off post-acquisition, but HP has yet to show a strong commitment to the PPM market, except as an adjunct to its primary products in testing and operations.
- The original product team eroded as a result of the HP acquisition of Mercury, aside from a few key roles directly responsible for continued PPM product development and marketing.

This portion translates as follows:

- Delivery is lagging behind schedule.
- HP is not putting full force behind the market offering, apparently due to a focus in other areas.
- Many of the key players have jumped ship.

We would say that this is typical of the M&A scenario. A big company buys a small company to get something that it doesn't have or cannot create for itself economically. The deal gets done, key people leave, delivery performance suffers, and service levels drop. That is a strong mixture of ingredients that leads to value loss. And it does not have to be this way. Sometimes, after reviewing the options, a company's best decision is to avoid merger or acquisition because of considerations of the people, process, and technology matched with the strategy of the company.

As an example, in 1997, CabCo was entering the rack business in data centers. Racks are the cabinets that hold computing and power supply equipment in a standard design. Rack manufacturers can differentiate themselves on construction details, strength, weight, cooling characteristics, ease of assembly, and so on, but all must conform to standard mounting patterns for equipment. One of CabCo's competitors was beginning to bundle racks with power conditioning equipment. This was a competitive threat to CabCo. Without being able to offer the same bundle while continuing to provide only the power equipment, CabCo stood to lose a significant share of the market. Therefore, the question became whether to create rack manufacturing capability, acquire a company that had the capability, or come up with some other solution. Up until this point, CabCo had been able to satisfy its needs by purchasing racks from a company in Europe. This solution was not going to last because of the cost pressure in the marketplace. CabCo had to make a choice either to play in this space with a low-cost solution or to suffer the market share loss. What CabCo did was look at the options available to it and noticed the following:

- Differentiation came from rack design, not manufacturing cost.
- There were multiple options for getting a rack manufactured once it was designed.
- Multiple businesses could be acquired that had the manufacturing capability, most of which were in Asia.
- The core competencies were rack design and business-to-business marketing.

Taking into account the costs of acquisition, the relative advantage of owning in-house capability, and the nonacquisition options open to it, CabCo elected to develop its own in-house design expertise, develop its business-to-business marketing capability, and purchase outsourced rack manufacturing service from an Asian supplier. Over time, this proved to be a far better way to approach the rack business because it blended the best in-house capability with the best outsourced economy.

Unfortunately, the way M&As can be driven by the pursuit of top line revenue, company size, or operational cost "synergy" can create a significant cost of acquisition without real return, as well as unnecessary ongoing risks. For instance, if CabCo had owned the rack manufacturer, it would have not only incurred the costs of integration of the people of the acquired business but also taken on the risk of losses as demand for racks fluctuates. Sometimes the best merger is the one that does not happen. But as we will see later on in this chapter, there are very strong forces pushing for mergers even when they make no sense.

In other cases, the merger makes perfect sense, but the integration destroys value. In 1998, TopCo bought CordCo, a company that made large power supply components in a different product family from TopCo's products. TopCo could not create the capability easily, but needed to if it was to penetrate the systems market that it had bet the company on.

In the case of CordCo, TopCo took the approach of sending in its team to make changes in the way CordCo operated, immediately after the acquisition. Among many fast and furious changes made in the integration of the two businesses, there were major shifts in service organizations, and satellite offices were closed. Whereas TopCo operated from a standard product model, CordCo was designed to do mostly custom work. The changes in the service organization and the office closings destroyed the means by which CordCo created value for its customers. TopCo's view of the world was based on products, not solutions. Forcing the product model of TopCo over the solution model of CordCo proved costly. The result was a destruction of most of the value in the CordCo company acquisition. It took several years to recover from the effects of this integration gone bad.

In the CordCo acquisition, TopCo also got one of CordCo's subsidiaries, called BarCo. Fortunately, an entirely different approach was taken with BarCo. BarCo made large-scale systems for industrial, military, and utility customers. During the acquisition, the CTO of CordCo highly recommended that BarCo be allowed to remain a wholly owned subsidiary. Because TopCo knew how little it knew about the BarCo business model, it left BarCo separate. Only after several years were changes made to bring BarCo on to company systems and operations. Up until then, BarCo remained untouched. In the acquisition of TopCo by AtCo, BarCo was found to be a close match for the industrial segment of AtCo, which added value to the TopCo acquisition. The value of BarCo in retrospect could easily have been destroyed by using the same approach with BarCo as with CordCo.

What may not be clear from these examples is that the decision process for how to handle the CordCo integration was the same process used to decide how to handle BarCo—with very different results. The company used basic gut feel to execute the integration or not to integrate at all. At the time, there was no knowledge in the company as to how integration should be handled, which left the company guessing as to the best way to proceed. We suspect that many companies approach integration in a less than thoughtful way with regard to the organizational DNA of the two entities. What we aspire to in this chapter is to provide straightforward suggestions as to how you can improve the decision-making process and capture maximum value in the M&A area. One of us had a boss who was fond of saying "Learn from others' mistakes because you don't have time to make them all yourself." Our hope is that the following lessons will save you some time, money, and frustration.

Lesson 1: Deals Come First, Cleanup Comes Second (Unfortunately)

Many of the organizational issues that are likely to erode or destroy value are knowable ahead of time. Many ill-advised deals can be seen from a long distance away. It is easy to see the merger disasters beforehand, but there is a part of the M&A system that prevents the application of reasonable analysis to such situations. Whereas there is extreme focus on the search for synergies and the contracting and agreement documentation, culture integration is not typically included in the merger planning budget. It is much harder to get the budget approved for cultural assessment and workforce integration analysis and planning. In our experience, where the focus on people integration is part of the merger plan and budget, the merger process is much more successful, but such "people work" is still almost always done after the fact. Our suggestion is that organizations not only put the culture integration into the merger budget but also include it in the decision-making process for approving the merger in the first place. There is often no way to clean up merger failures after the fact. Volumes have been written about how mergers destroy value. Amazingly, there were few articles ahead of the merger that pointed out the obvious disconnect between the companies.

It is difficult to tell a decision maker that culture, which is messy, is critical to merger success. Numbers in financial analysis are a lot easier to validate than a conflict in culture. The burden of proof in numbers that can be added and subtracted is much easier to deal with than trying to prove the impact of the clash in cultures. Equally difficult to prove beyond a reasonable doubt are the conflicts of purpose, long-range intention, identity, driving metrics and incentives, goals, structure, and fundamental strategy. Thus it becomes a matter of comparing that which can be demonstrated clearly in numbers to that which can be demonstrated in concept and case study. In our experience, the numbers win most of the time. There is very little rocket science in conducting the organizational assessment that could ultimately save the enterprise from a merger disaster, but most leadership teams do not avail themselves of the information and take action accordingly.

Aside from the difficulties associated with looking at the organizational issues, there is the fear that if executives actually did so, the deal might be squelched. Notice that at the point of failure, the lawyers, the accounting firms, and the consultants have all been paid. The outgoing executive team has put their cash in the bank and moved on to the next chapter. So who is holding the bag? The current shareholders. For anyone who has flown over Las Vegas, it becomes obvious how much capital can be generated from people losing money in a casino and paying for entertainment. There are a multitude of multibillion-dollar structures erected using gamblers' money. The same is true for the M&A arena. Many of the skyscrapers that have been built to hold the legal, accounting, and finance empires in our financial centers have been funded by money taken from the transactions of companies being bought and sold. It is a bit ironic that an industry with a 70 percent failure rate can live so well. No other could withstand that degree of poor quality and survive.

What is clear is that there is a significant problem in a decision-making system that leaves out critical information that must be considered to make a merger a success. In our experience, it would be better to pass on a few deals than to ignore the obvious disconnects between organizations prior to attempting to merge them.

M&A teams need to spend the time and budget for due diligence on the human capital side of the enterprise with the same intensity as they do for the financial side. This is one of the reasons that the HR organizations of the world must rise to the challenge of being a true strategic partner. In some organizations, HR is a full partner in the M&A scene. In others, HR is an afterthought. Part of any improvement in merger success rates will come from creating better organizational integration strategies that include structural design, culture integration, metric design, incentive design, and the movement of key people in, around, and out of the organization. Looking forward, it may take some time for organizations to be proactive about the organizational issues of M&As. In the meantime, moving as fast as possible on the heels of the deal clos-ing is going to be the best bet for minimizing damage and maxi-mizing the value capture where organizations are being combined.

Lesson 2: Connect the Dots Between Mergers and Transformation

In executing business transformation, mergers are a means to a transformational end. The key is to connect M&A activity to specific transformational benefit or impact. What follows is a set of potential reasons for merger and some considerations as to their transformational value versus their organizational risk.

Reason 1: Taking out a competitor. We are not talking about creating a monopoly. What we are getting at is that transforming a company from a strong competitor to a dominant player in a market may involve acquiring a company to consolidate the industry. The risk is that because the target company was a competitor, the merger could be rather hostile, and the value lost in the process may offset the gain in the market.

Reason 2: Gaining a technology. It is common for a company to acquire other companies to gain access to a technology that it would take years to develop on its own. To bring in the new technology, the retention of the right people to go with the tech-nology itself is often critical. Adding technology can be very transformational to a company, but it will do no good if the inno-vation that produced the technology is destroyed in the process of acquiring it.

Reason 3: Top line growth. Bigger is better unless bigger creates disproportionate risk. Taking the biggest risk are organizations that make the commitment to acquire another organization but neglect to account thoroughly for the infrastructure required to fully integrate the acquisition. It sometimes sounds great to add to the size of the organization—until the reality of incompatible systems, outdated competencies, and incoherent strategies sets in. If the reason for the acquisition is size for the sake of size, we suggest that organizations think again. Transformation is about creating a better enterprise, not simply a bigger one.

Reason 4: Added capacity. Achieving economy of scale means to spread fixed costs over larger volumes, yielding higher margins. If transformation is targeted at efficiencies and economies, making acquisitions that create expanded capacity can be a great transformational move. The key here is to make sure that the move toward greater manufacturing capacity is matched with sales, distribution, and service capacity. Otherwise, the transformation may be toward a more unwieldy enterprise as opposed to a more efficient one.

Reason 5: Access to markets. Sometimes the best way to develop channels is to buy them. If an organization is aiming to be a global player, merger may be the best way to go global. Right after the merger check clears, however, it may dawn on the leadership team that they now have teams of people in countries they do not understand, an HR organization that is unprepared for international labor law, and communication systems that no longer cover the needs of the business. Making sure that the entire investment is made in the transformation to cover cost of ownership of the new entity becomes critical.

Reason 6: Specific people of a specific competency. One of the tricky parts of acquiring a professional services organization is that the asset value is hard to borrow against. In other words, the exact value of intellectual property that has not been converted to documents, processes, patents, and other forms of tangible property is hard to determine. However, it may be that the exact transformational asset that is needed is actually the brainpower of specific individuals. In this case, the merger must be designed using more people factors than financial factors. This makes bankers and lawyers nervous because there is no way to compel someone to perform or to cooperate. If there is no way to do so, it makes the absolute value of assets nearly impossible to compute. Nothing makes a numbers person more uneasy than things that don't respond to math. Therefore, a focus on organizational issues may be needed, and more people from the nonnumerical part of the business need to weigh in.

Reason 7: Buying to learn or to spark innovation. Sometimes organizations legitimately and honestly want to change their ways. Perhaps the organization has stopped being innovative in its space, so acquiring an organization with an innovative spirit would help the parent organization be more innovative. Our advice in these situations would be to save the cost of acquisition and do something else with the money. An established organization that has stopped innovating will slowly and surely wrap its bureaucratic, control-oriented, noncollaborative boa constrictor body around the new acquisition and squeeze the life out of it. One by one, the innovators will find new pastures. When a critical mass of what made the company innovative has left, innovation will cease to exist. The process is irreversible and irrecoverable. The best hope for the preservation of innovation is structural separation between the acquired entity and the "mother ship."

In the process of transforming an organization, M&As have a substantial role to play. What we are suggesting is that a direct relationship be drawn between the merger activity and the transformational benefit to be derived. When people begin to suggest that the dots get connected between the merger and transformation, they run the career risk of going against the grain of all the people who will benefit from the transaction going through. They must fight the tendencies to cut such analysis and forethought out of the budget and to fear running afoul of powerful people who do not want to hear such things.

Lesson 3: Watch Out for Synergies

Mergers always look good on paper. After all, if the numbers were not favorable, if there were documented evidence that the merger is a loser, why would anyone move forward? But the reality is often very different from the plan. The headcount that will be saved, the economies of management, the spans of control, and the consolidation of factories all point to prosperity in the plan, but when the completed merger is evaluated, the benefits realized are often disappointing.

There are a few major factors to consider when exploring synergies. First, it is important to determine who has accountability for the actual as opposed to planned synergies. Many times, the person doing the synergy estimate is going to be long gone when the estimate becomes a reality. We suggest that organizations establish accountability for tracking and set performance targets. This means that the person doing the estimating and presentation of the synergy in the initial stages of the merger must establish agreed-on performance criteria as part of creating the synergy estimate. You should also examine the assumptions under these estimates. The risk associated with the assumptions is the risk of having the estimate be over or under the nominal value. No synergy estimate should be accepted without a thorough examination of the assumptions on which it is based with an associated risk analysis of the assumptions.

One element of being accountable for synergy estimates is to identify the boundary conditions that represent the best-case, most likely, and worst-case estimates. Ask for a sensitivity analysis based on multipoint estimates. Risk comes in ranges, not in numbers. The merger must make sense at the boundary conditions, not just in the nominal or best-case scenario. Estimates are exactly that—estimates. They have an equal chance of being over or under a nominal value. What appears to be going on in the world of mergers is that synergies are committed at the best-case end of the range of outcomes, and the actual values are coming in at a much lower spot. Some of this is to be expected. After all, it wouldn't be called *risk* if it always turned out positive. That being said, we can do a much better job of eliminating some of the nonsense around synergies that commonly takes place.

Lesson 4: Compare the DNA of the Two Organizations Being Merged

Some of the difficulties in mergers can be avoided with a careful look at how the merging organizations developed into their present state of being. When we look at mergers that fail, what stands out is the major difference in operating philosophy. Daimler is known for its depth of engineering. Chrysler has long been a company that focused on design innovation. The idea of creating the retro cars Prowler, Viper, and PT Cruiser is as foreign to Daimler as the idea of producing cars for the Autobahn is to Chrysler. These differences translate into operating difficulties as the conflicts with regard to product design, product development road maps, marketing, and sales lead to compromised decision making. The roots and traditions of each organization drive very different mental models, and each holds on to its position as if it were a matter of survival. That is because it *is* a matter of survival—survival of the ideas, values, processes, events, and actions that have made each organization what it is today.

People give up on their ideals neither easily nor quickly, if ever. Therefore, it is critical in the early stages of a merger to assess and act on the basic elements of DNA that form the foundation of the enterprises that are being combined. What needs to be preserved is the enterprise value that is embedded in people. If the merger or acquisition is strictly or mostly technical in nature, where the preservation of the people and their tacit knowledge is unimportant, the following does not apply. But if the value of the merger or acquisition is heavily dependent on the retention of people and their motivation, what we discuss here is critical. There are eight primary attributes that when mapped to compare the companies will show fundamental alignment or misalignment, allowing executive teams to take concrete action to minimize collateral damage in the process of M&A.

Attribute 1: Purpose

According to Nikos Mourkogiannis, the author of *Purpose* (Palgrave Macmillan, 2007), an organization primarily dedicates itself to a purpose in one of four areas:

1. Discovery—finding new ways of doing things
2. Excellence—doing things in an exemplary way even if not new
3. Heroism—saving the day for some group of stakeholders
4. Altruism—service to the masses

The nature of the mapping challenge here is to identify the historic and current emphasis placed on each of these aspects of fundamental purpose. Our experience tells us that organizations exhibit all four types of purpose and emphasize one or two, but are not exclusively dedicated to one. If the emphasized purposes of the two organizations being merged differ substantially, the tension created by the difference will likely be a source of conflict until understood and resolved. It is critical to know the pattern that purpose has taken in an organization because it is the source of intrinsic motivation that shapes the company. If there is a significant difference in the purpose of the two organizations being merged, it would be the basis for keeping them structurally separate or keeping the deal from moving forward.

Attribute 2: Identity

How an organization sees itself is as critical to its decision-making patterns as any other aspect of the organizational fabric. Seeing oneself as a health-creating organization is fundamentally different than seeing oneself as a pharmaceutical company. The former may make things that create health and well-being; the other may make drugs to treat the chronic and the acute. Not that there is anything inherently right or wrong about either one, but the two forced together can be toxic to one or the other or both. In mapping, it is critical to understand the prevailing view of the organization as to what it is, because this self-perception has a profound impact on the things people do naturally versus the things that they must force themselves to do. One of the best clues to this area is to map how the brand promise and brand image are articulated in each of the two enterprises.

Attribute 3: Long-Range Intention

Stating goals is often difficult for organizations. Long-range intention is one step beyond goal setting. It is the declaration of your "meta-goal," or the goal of your goals. To use a pharmaceutical industry example, there is a difference in long-range intention between seeking a cure for cancer and reaching the global market for the treatment of cancer. The former is focused on eradication of the disease itself; the second, on market share and distribution coverage. The point here is not to make one view or the other right or wrong but to create an understanding of how two organizations view their world and their intentions. People can be deeply insulted if you question their intentions. That insult may be compounded by superimposing a conflicting intention. This may explain the "allergic reactions" people have to being acquired by or merged with another enterprise.

Attribute 4: Culture

We have found William E. Schneider's and Geoffrey Moore's concepts of collaboration, control, cultivation, and competence to be useful in comparing organizations' cultures. (See, for example, Schneider's *The Reengineering Alternative* or Moore's *Dealing with Darwin* or *Living on the Fault Line*.) It is also possible to map using Geert Hofstede's models (see *Cultures and Organizations: Software of the Mind*) or any of a number of ways of viewing culture, but however you do it, focusing on the cultural aspects that determine decision making and group membership are critical.

Attribute 5: Structure

In the premerged organizations, each had a structure it used to get results. It could have been functionally oriented, as in silos or stovepipes, or it could have been very project-oriented. In most cases, there is a combination of both, but there is often one primary way that the organization distributes its power. Either the power goes primarily to the vertical elements of functions or to the horizontal elements of solution delivery. Each has its advantages, but the question is now about how the two organizations have been operating structurally.

Attribute 6: Goals

How organizations arrive at, declare, communicate, and track goals is critical to understanding how the leadership of each organization has functioned historically. In mapping goals, what you are looking for are the goals that drive organizational growth, which are different from the obvious downstream outcomes of profit, margins, market share, PE ratio, and so on.

Attribute 7: Metrics

Every organization has a set of formal or informal metrics that it pays the most attention to. The metrics could be regionally based revenue, product line profit, business unit profitability, net promoter score, installation defect free, cost per available seat mile, earnings before interest and taxes, or any of dozens of potential measurements. In mapping metrics for the purposes of analyzing the merging of enterprises, it is critical to map the two or three metrics the organization holds near and dear that define its performance.

Attribute 8: Strategic Approach

Organizations can dedicate themselves to only a finite number of things. Michael Porter has argued for decades (see, for example, "What Is Strategy?" *Harvard Business Review* 74, no. 6 [1996]:

61–78) that there are two fundamental strategies—cost leadership and differentiation—and that these two strategies require two separate approaches to business. In mapping organizational DNA, it becomes important to understand the means by which cost leadership is achieved or the nature of the differentiation. Perhaps one organization has historically been a cost leader and merges with a differentiator. If both are differentiated but one organization differentiates through channels of distribution and the other through product features and functions, it is equally challenging to get the organizations to merge effectively.

Example Comparison Summary

The table here is a high-level comparison of two companies. It is a simplification of a much larger analysis conducted over two days with an executive team. What it illustrates is the contrast between two successful enterprises and highlights the differences in the way each organization has created its success.

Parameter	Company A	Company B
Basis of purpose	Heroics	Excellence
Basis of long-range vision	Smart buildings	Service annuity
Identity	Product solutions	Service solutions
Cultural emphasis	Competence	Control-collaboration
Structure	Flat matrix	Flat matrix
Strategy basis	Product differentiation	Service differentiation
Goal emphasis	Grow	Grow if profitable
Key driving metric	Company-level growth	Region-level profit

In reviewing the comparison in the table, there are a few things that stand out. First of all, Company A is very determined to be a leader in products that are on the bleeding edge of innovation. The greater the emphasis on entering new markets with new technology the better, as far as Company A is concerned. People in this organization live and breathe for the next exciting way of delivering a knockout product. Company B, in contrast, is more interested in creating service contracts for larger and larger accounts that will be partners over the long term. For this company, products are the reason for the service contract, not a means to technological breakthrough. A solution sale with a long service contract is very appealing to Company B.

The merger presents the following difficulties:

- Product development strategy: the argument will be about whether to invest in cutting-edge products or to develop good-enough products that are conducive to service offerings.
- Brand messaging and brand merger strategy: the organizations' contrasting identities cause their brands to differ; what brand takes precedence and the brand messaging will be debated.
- Level of risk in the development portfolio: companies that are very discovery-oriented are going to want a focus on cutting-edge products and innovation; in contrast, a service orientation drives a focus on extended service offerings. The two will conflict when it comes to deciding where the development dollars are going to be spent.
- Pricing and service-level agreements: Company A's emphasis on growth will push for lower-margin products to gain share, whereas Company B's emphasis on regional profit will push for higher margins and more lucrative service-level agreements.

Under these circumstances, the leaders must decide what is to be preserved and what is to be sacrificed in the process of merging two enterprises of such different DNA. This is an opportunity for leaders to clarify what the intention of the merger is and plan accordingly. If the two organizations are simply pushed together, one of the DNA strands will eventually dominate—assuming it does not cause the organization to fail due to internal conflicts.

Leaders should choose one of the sets of characteristics to be preserved and let the other naturally fade away over time. Selecting leaders who can reshape the organization based on the DNA of the future enterprise will enable the desired DNA to become dominant. The DNA of the current organization will gradually fade in influence. This is much easier in the case of a large organization acquiring a small organization than it is for a "merger of equals." In all probability, Daimler and Chrysler cultures would never merge into one. In contrast, when HP, IBM, or Cisco makes twenty-plus acquisitions in a year, the relative size of the two enterprises being merged makes conversion of the DNA much easier.

Leaders should also consider keeping the two organizations structurally separate so that they maintain their characteristics. In the same way that Cisco keeps some of its acquisitions separate (Scientific Atlanta and LinkSys, for example), the merged organization can benefit by integrating only back-office operations and keeping the rest of the organization structurally separate so that the conflicts in DNA are prevented. When much of the value of the acquisition is in the specific people involved, this is the lowest-risk strategy to preserve value in the process of acquisition. Only by keeping the DNA intact through structural separation will the risk of losing critical skills be mitigated.

This simple example of comparing the DNA of two organizations on a high level illustrates how one can expose the sources of significant merger issues. Notice that the subject of financial synergies is not part of this discussion, yet most of the integration activity in a typical merger is placed on balance sheets and income statements. The simple truth is that no matter what the balance sheets say, the value of the deal is going to hinge on the people, not the accounting. What we are saying is that the typical M&A activity is massively out of balance in favor of the numbers and at the expense of people; the value lost as a consequence of this imbalance causes the merger not to reach its numbers. It is as if focusing on the numbers is the best way to underperform on the numbers.

Lesson 5: Don't Change That Which You Do Not Understand

In 2001, PartCo was losing sales because it did not have a package offer of integrated components. At that point, PartCo was a products company, and it wanted to be a solutions company. The best way to achieve this was to acquire the pieces the company did not have. PartCo made a cash offer to a company called FloCo, and the deal was done. Almost. FloCo was a company whose DNA was built to create custom-engineered solutions. PartCo was a company that was built on the idea of configuring orders from standard hardware. The DNA of the two companies was vastly different, but that did not keep PartCo from imposing the configuration model on top of the customization model. In the process, PartCo created an 80 percent loss in revenue in just the first two years of operation. Most of the value that was contained in the people who knew how the business ran was lost as the company was cut down to a handful of people who were absorbed into PartCo. No company is likely to create this kind of value disaster by direct intent. However, disaster is quite likely in any given merger unless a measure of caution is taken to begin to execute change based on an understanding of the underlying systems and concepts that made the acquisition attractive in the first place.

If the acquiring company does not understand the reasons for the acquisition's success, it should not alter what is working until it does. The merger might be based on economies, but being more efficient at a dramatic loss in revenue is hardly the target. If leaders truly understand the profit value chain of a company, it becomes easier to make changes that guard the workings of what makes the company successful. Without looking at this, leaders will find it all too easy to make assumptions that do not bear out in fact and create the effect we see in the FloCo example. At FloCo, the abilities to create custom, short-lead-time orders and do work on a bid-spec level were critical. Both critical pieces of the business model were destroyed in forcing the configuration model on the company.

Strategy mapping helps identify the customer outcomes that are optimized by the company for the customer and the customer's customer. This is an adjunct to profit value chain analysis and provides the insight required to be able to change the company while protecting the unique selling proposition that made the company worth acquiring in the first place.

A company's social network, which drives how and when things get done, is a precious asset. Not everything that counts in keeping an operation humming along and producing is codified to a system or documented in a process. It is critical to identify the set of individuals who hold the key knowledge and relationships in the business. Not understanding how this network is constructed and who the players are can be the beginning of a major setback. Taking the wrong cut to save money, a cut that destroys critical social networks, is to risk a significant destruction of value.

Lesson 6: Deal with Free Radicals Head-On

What happens when a company is acquired by another company and the key intellectual assets just don't seem to mesh with the combined enterprise? What do we mean by intellectual assets? They are the least accounted for and most precious asset of a knowledge-based company. They are the people who know how the company really works. They are the people who were the reason that the company was worth buying in the first place. You will not find them on the balance sheet. There will be no mention of them on the asset inventory. No dollar value is associated with them directly, even though all the dollar value of the organization is a result of their actions and decisions. If these people leave or if they remain but disengage their creative energy, the company stands to lose a great deal of future value. If they remain in the postmerger enterprise, we call these disengaged individuals *free radicals*. They are still free to do their jobs, but are somewhat radical in their relationship to the combined enterprise.

Our direct observation tells us that the postmerger organization's approach to its free radicals is critical to its success. Most mergers take intellectual assets into account by way of financial incentives and golden parachutes. Often, people have some financial reason to stay with the enterprise. The problem is that their loyalty and their best creative energy are not for sale. Consider that these people were successful in the old enterprise. That is why they were acquired. But often the new enterprise does not see the need to listen to them. After all, it is the acquiring company. It knows what is best. Except where it doesn't.

A significant problem arises when the acquiring company is of a different core, including a different purpose, a different identity, and a different long-range intention than the one that the free radicals came from. This creates an environment where a storm is not far off. A sort of Darwinian process of natural selection begins, determining who will stay and who will leave. Will the free radicals cause the new acquirer to adapt to them? Will the new acquirer cause them to adapt? Both? Neither? This becomes pivotal because free radicals are typically too wise and too capable simply to roll over and play dead.

Here are the alternatives: (1) the free radicals get on the new bandwagon, (2) they remain free radicals in an organization whose antibodies begin to isolate them for extraction, (3) they reinvent themselves, (4) they cause a reinvention of the enterprise, or (5) they move on to do something that they like and feel passionate about where they can get what they want.

If the strategy of the new enterprise depends on the retention of the free radicals, a leadership intervention is the only thing that will prevent a catastrophic loss of talent and therefore a loss of strategic options. People contribute their best when they work from their core. If the core of the free radical becomes incompatible with the new enterprise, the best thing a free radical can do is exit. Incompatibility is not hard to measure. Frustration level, stress level, and bottom-line positive emotional response versus negative response to being in the organization are the best metrics for free radicals to gauge their direction. This is not to suggest an "If it feels good, do it" strategy, but we have to ask why talented people would be willing to contribute long term to a cause they do not feel passionate about.

Many acquisitions lose value because the free radicals who are strategically critical are not given enough consideration in the transaction. In business, we have progressed far beyond the acquisition of factories, equipment, and fields. We now acquire human networks. Yet our M&A processes, systems, and post-merger leadership are still stuck back in the days of trucks and tractors as if people were completely fungible.

To acquiring companies, we say: pay attention to the non-balance-sheet assets ... they are what you really paid for.

To free radicals, we say: adapt and stay or quit and leave, but do not quit and stay ... your energy is best utilized where it does not involve tilting against windmills.

Summary

Transformation will continue to require mergers. Mergers will always cause some level of transformation. The two are permanently linked. In the process of merger, however, organizations have a long way to go to improve a rather dismal record of performance relative to the preservation of value. Central to improvement is the expansion of focus on the organizational integration aspect of M&As. How people are accounted for intellectually, personally, and emotionally in the plans for M&As is critical and yet often bungled in a rush to get the deal done based on the numbers. Much of this is brought on by a conflict of interest on the part of all the significant decision-making entities in the merger process. Only through careful consideration of the longer-term interest of shareholders and stakeholders of the enterprise will organizations make progress in improving the process of selecting companies with which to merge and with which not to merge.

Ten Key Questions

1. Do you consider the risks of merger integration before making a deal?

2. Do you know how to assess and mitigate those risks?

3. Did your last merger consider integration issues early on or before the deal was made?

4. Do you have an integration plan that includes the human factors in the integration?

5. Have the synergies of merger been overstated?

6. Do you have a way of knowing what the synergies really were?

7. Did you compare the DNA of the two organizations?

8. Are you at risk of changing things you do not understand?

9. Have you dealt effectively with free radicals?

10. Do you have the ability to apply lessons from past mergers to future merger activity?

10

WHO MELTED MY CHEESE?

What to Do When Two Companies Merge Different Recipes

IBM buys Lotus, Tata buys Jaguar, Cisco buys Scientific Atlanta and LinkSys, Daimler buys Chrysler. Sometimes the big fish eats the small fish; sometimes it is a merger of equals. In any event, mergers are rarely profitable. Although estimates vary, most express the value of mergers in general in negative numbers. It remains somewhat of a mystery as to why merger mania continues when evidence shows that most mergers degrade long-term value and negatively impact people. Although companies that grow through many acquisitions tend to perform better than those that don't, one could also question whether the performance increase is because of the mergers or in spite of them.

Whether the merger is profitable or not, what we are talking about here is what to *do* during a merger. It is difficult to know or predict what will happen when two cultures mix. Even though the product road maps may look compatible, when the culture of one company becomes the property of a company whose culture is different, the difference creates a severe challenge. The people who found meaning in their company of origin find limited satisfaction in coming to work for an organization that doesn't value the same things. Not that the acquiring organization is wrong—it's just different. The old expression "The thrill is gone" does not suffice to express the emotion people feel when they experience something that is not what they were getting up for in the morning.

One result of mergers that we have observed is the creation of free radicals, whom we introduced in Chapter Nine. Free radicals are people who are disconnected from the culture of the acquiring organization and don't adapt to and adopt the new culture and direction. For these people, staying is difficult unless they have such tight golden handcuffs that they cannot realistically make a change. They may be of an age and skill set that make changing employers more problematic than staying at a company where they are unhappy. But whether the impossibility of leaving is real or imagined, it affects their job performance. Organizations often react by isolating these individuals and making their position irrelevant, but this can be very damaging to the company and to people.

Having to deal with free radicals is just one of the people-related issues that have a severe impact on the success of mergers. In many cases, people issues get set aside in the early stages of the merger process, only to emerge as the central issues in getting the merged enterprise to perform. In one case of a large merger, approximately 40 percent of the value of the enterprises burned up in the process of forging the merger. Tragically, the preconditions of this type of toxic mixture are easily identified and almost never integrated into the premerger analysis.

The reality is, no company is immune to mergers. M&A is part of corporate reality, and mergers are likely to accelerate in today's climate. In fact, as valuations of targets become cheaper by the day, larger companies who have managed themselves well in the current financial crisis will be assembling their shopping lists of companies to acquire. For cash-rich organizations or those with access to capital, most targets are on the bargain rack. Firms that were once considered immovable independent institutions, such as Merrill Lynch, have been and will be acquired. Because every company is a little different, preparation for a merger is impossible without knowing specifically whom the merger is with.

M&As present huge challenges to an organization's culture and people. What seemed like a great idea at first turns into a major headache as the two organizations attempt to get work done. Aside from dealing with different systems, processes, and business practices, staff from acquired companies must learn to speak a whole new language—not French or Chinese, but the business language of the new parent. On a deeper level, employees of the acquired company may feel they are losing their identity and their motivation for coming to work.

Overcoming these hurdles to working together requires more than symbolic gestures. On the day of one merger announcement, European employees were served donuts as a symbol of their merger with an American company; the American staff were served German pastries. Unfortunately, cultural integration cannot happen by swapping breakfast menus. In fact, this type of symbolic ritual can create more cynicism than it could possibly be worth. When the overall integration is poorly planned and executed, symbolic gestures can be insulting.

Adding to the stress of the merger is the identity crisis resulting from the discussion of which entity was the victor and which was the vanquished. Acquiring companies tend to establish themselves as top dog and expect the employees of the acquired company simply to adopt their existing culture and business practices. What ensues is a train wreck of cultures that manifests itself both overtly and in more subtle ways. People can publicly support what they privately resent, but sooner or later, the resentment will emerge. Stephen Covey pointed out years ago (*Seven Habits of Highly Effective People*, New York: Simon & Schuster, 1989) that unexpressed feelings never really die, but are simply buried alive and come forward later in bigger and uglier ways.

Managing the collision of cultures is not just important, it is critical to survival. The biggest challenge is dealing with the free radicals, those employees who can't seem to adapt to the new environment. These free radicals are cancerous to a company's survival; swift and sure steps must be taken to deal with the situation before it creates damage. Luckily, much can be done to prevent the creation of free radicals.

Actively Engage with People

Employees have real fears, hopes, concerns, and questions after a merger or acquisition. Whether these feelings are real to you or not, they are real to the people experiencing them. People need a great deal of support to be able to cope with the uncertainty of the postmerger environment, which is a cost not identified in the numerical analysis of the merger. This period of anxiety is completely normal and to be expected. Managers will need to dedicate large periods of time to one-on-one "therapy" sessions with affected employees. People need to know what their role will be in the merged enterprise. If they can understand their new role, they have something to put their energy into. Without this understanding, the period of limbo is torture. In a postmerger environment, people can feel as if they are on hold, but if they have some way to actively engage, the period of anxiety will be much shorter.

In order to make the merger less painful, it is important to avoid propagating negative information about the situation and the acquiring organization. One of us was present at HP headquarters during the time of the HP split that created Agilent. After the announcement about the split had been made, an employee of HP indicated that the word "Agilent" sounded to him a lot like *flatulent*. The capacity of people to transform almost anything into a negative should not be underestimated. It happens quickly and must be coached aggressively.

The process of merger integration is a long one. What counts is the development of strength in the longer term. It is important to avoid launching battles about ways of doing things. The way things are done in terms of the content and sequence of processes, what work gets done, and what work product is produced—this is culture in action. When two companies merge, you can expect that people are going to have strong reactions to changes in the way work gets done because it is the carrier of culture and may have strong implications and deep roots. But time wasted in bickering over the best way to do something can mean a missed opportunity to improve customer value. Before anyone gets out his or her shovel and begins to dig in, leaders need to suspend the argument until an opportunity to make an improvement presents itself. Otherwise, turf wars can break out at the expense of productive effort.

Cultivate a New Identity and Purpose

The newly combined entity has the opportunity for a fresh new perspective on what it wants to become. Take the opportunity to become something special and unique to your customers and employees. You don't necessarily have to ask the newly acquired organization to emulate the new mother ship. Contrary to the way announcements are made, your goal is not to meet in the middle, compromise, get consensus, or "take the best of both companies." Although the idea of taking the best of both worlds may sound appealing and intellectually pleasing, it doesn't always work in real organizations. The best-of-both-worlds concept is largely a myth. We might like the product line of one company and the structure of another, but that does not mean that we can get the product line we like produced in the structure we admire. If this were a natural occurrence, HP-Compaq and AOL Time Warner would have been marriages made in heaven. Instead, they are somewhere between mediocre and terrible. The goal should not be to create a blend but rather to create a new entity that may be closer to either one or the other company, or a completely different company altogether.

The first step is to create a vision of what you want to become. This should be something new and not simply a combination of what both companies once were. Second, let people in the newly acquired company contribute positively to the culture, not just accept the one that was there to begin with. Third, encourage employees to uncover and define specific projects and opportunities for process improvement, people development, innovation, collaboration, cost reduction, market expansion, customer loyalty, or other improvements that are now possible with the new capabilities of the combined companies. And fourth, build new teams with members from both sides. This will bring new blood, new life, and new perspectives to teams. Engaging people in collaborative projects is the best way to engage cultural integration. But be careful not to poison any magic formulas or competitive advantages just for the sake of cross-pollination.

This approach can help build a platform for transformation. It will eliminate the distraction of squabbling over whose model was better than the other or who was better at one thing or the other. A new purpose lets both sides forget the past and look to the future. If the engagement of people is handled correctly, employees from both the acquired and acquiring companies should feel as though they are working for a new and different company. Ultimately a new culture can only emerge by way of people learning to be successful in getting things done.

Create a Detailed Integration Plan for Teams to Rally Around

Develop a revised integration strategy that mirrors the original strategic intent for the acquisition, but that now contains the input from the acquired company. Remember that the newly acquired company may have new ideas that make the integration strategy even stronger. Then develop a revised detailed integration work plan based on the new integration strategy. Try to make the plan as comprehensive as possible, even in areas that may seem unaffected by the acquisition, such as specialized sales or product development. Involving most of the teams in the company will ensure that everyone is moving in the same direction.

Make sure the integration plan is aligned with the new purpose for being, as described in the previous section. The integration plan is your way to get on track to the new purpose. Don't create organizations and teams that are defined by the companies they worked for before the acquisition. Such an approach will maintain silos, limit the advantages of the combined companies, and avoid or delay true integration.

Be sure to quantify integration goals and set aggressive timetables to achieve them. Teams will feel motivated once objectives are clear. Form teams that are composed of people from both premerged entities. Make sure they collaborate on plans to achieve goals. It is the best way to establish new normative behaviors that are consistent with getting good results. There is little point in philosophical discussions about culture integration. Focus on getting something accomplished, and the cultural norms associated with performance will form naturally. Get everybody on the same systems as quickly as possible. Allocate sufficient budget for systems integration projects. Failure to do this frustrates people and destroys productivity.

Define new business processes that are standard for the entire new organization. This will limit confusion about how to get things done in the new environment. Use manual approaches until everything can be automated, as opposed to letting old processes and systems linger.

Standardize roles and responsibilities across teams from both sides. Wherever practical, use new names for roles so that the people from one company do not feel that they are simply being forced to deploy the roles of the other. For example, if one company had called its outside salespeople "territory managers" and the other had used "district representatives," then use "district manager" or some other completely new name for the role going forward.

Go Fast

Speed is an antidote for indecision. If an organization is given large amounts of time, there is no end to what it can invent as reasons for not moving on. The best way to demonstrate leadership is to do so with a quick pace. The longer people languish in the postmerger haze, the more manifestations they can make about risk and other paralyzing thoughts. Following are some guidelines:

- Make any required layoffs or expense cuts once and quickly so that people can get past the basic fear of losing their job.
- Push teams to merge quickly, and they won't have time to complain, trash-talk, spread rumors, or even look for other jobs!
- Keep people busy for long enough, and before you know it, they will wake up inside a new company, fully integrated. They will have forgotten most of their concerns.
- Announce organizational structures, including the names of the people in the structure, quickly. But make sure to give consideration to qualified leaders from all sides before announcing management positions.
- Create teams with members from previously separate organizations.

Move On or Move Out

In mergers, power structures change, and so does the way people relate to the organization. Change in ownership of the company means a change in who has influence and who does not. One aspect of organizations that is seldom taken into account is the idea of social networks. In any given organization, there are people who have an extraordinary level of connectedness with others in the organization. These people exert disproportionate influence because they have the ability to control the flow of what information gets to what part of the organization. They largely control what goes on in an organization and how it does what it does. They are the central repository for tacit knowledge at critical places in the organization. Such people are central nodes in the network and have a huge number of connections that cannot be seen on the organization chart. However, the connections that central actors have are more critical than the lines and boxes on a typical organization chart. This is because influence really travels through the social network, not the lines and boxes. When a newly merged organization mishandles a person who has a central node position, it creates a problem. Because of her network strength, this individual holds significant power. If the direction of the merged enterprise conflicts with the person in a major way, she can become a free radical.

Care must be taken early in the integration to understand where the central nodes in the network are and what is going to be done to retain them or extract them from the business. Seek out the free radicals who will try to sabotage the new organization. Watch for those who are trash-talking or spreading ill will. The negative impact of a central node in the network is multiplied by the size of his network. The more central the actor, the more risk of damage there is from his becoming a free radical. Work with these individuals and give them a chance to engage and adapt. Seek ways to reconnect them and their network to the organization. Some will change and accept the new reality. Some will self-select for departure. The others must be quickly removed from the organization with the urgency of a surgeon removing a rapidly growing tumor. Managers must have the fortitude to exit these employees. Although these people may have been star players, their free radical status becomes a liability in the merged enterprise.

Dealing with free radicals is a significant job for HR as part of the integration team. If the HR organization cannot step up to the challenge of retention beyond designing the architecture of a monetary incentive plan, the merger is at risk of losing significant value as key knowledge workers turn off and tune out.

Communicate Like Crazy

Communicate, communicate, and communicate some more. If you're not sure you are communicating enough, you aren't doing enough. If you feel as though you're overcommunicating, you aren't, but you may be doing just enough. One of the biggest problems in times of organizational change can be loosely defined as poor communication. It is unlikely that it is a matter of input shortage; most people have more than enough incoming e-mail, voice mail, and text messages. The problem is more likely an inadequate supply of information that is in a form that allows people to know what to do. What people really need is to be able to translate all the high-level language of the organization into something that is actionable at their level. What people need to know falls into four categories, in the following order:

1. They need information that has to do with survival, such as layoffs, reduction of salary, plant closings, and the like. It is unlikely that you can capture anyone's attention about the lofty concepts of merger value if she fears for her livelihood.

2. They need information that deals with relationships—for instance, anything that has an impact on close relationships in the business that might affect their network.

3. They need to know about anything that involves opportunities moving forward, such as new technologies and new aspects of the organization that open the doors to growth and development.

4. They need to know why the organization is relevant, important, and unique. People need to be able to connect to something much larger than themselves in order to find an intrinsic sense of motivation.

If you think that you spotted a hierarchy of needs embedded in the four points here, you are entirely correct. People cannot hear a message that is at a higher level in the discussion hierarchy than the one that is most on their mind. It also follows that people won't hear a message about growth and opportunity if they think that the message at the survival level is a lie or a spin of some sort. So it is not only about communication but about credible information set out in a carefully crafted orchestration of complete information at all levels.

In addition to the four levels, it is important that you use all channels available to you in getting information out to people. Using single messages on one channel is far from adequate. Repeating messages as often as possible on as many channels as possible is critical. The following are actions that we have found helpful in communicating effectively.

- Bring small and large groups together for communicating new strategies, vision, and goals.
- Use multiple formats, including formal presentations, conference calls, town hall–style meetings, webcasts, dinners, parties, and small team meetings.
- Publish monthly newsletters or messages from the CEO. Include what's going on in different parts of the company.
- Make sure the parent company highlights the wins and successes of teams from the acquired company.
- Communicate new personal development, training, and career opportunities that didn't exist before.
- Highlight strengths of each former company and how each might help improve the other and shore up any weaknesses.
- Communicate what has been done to identify and surface issues quickly and get them resolved.
- Celebrate successes large and small to gain momentum.

Think of Mergers as Blended Families

Let us suppose that two families are about to merge. Both have several children and have been successful in their own right, but something has happened. Either through a death or divorce, they find themselves in a position that merging the two families is the next step to take. The top management (aka mom or dad) has decided that a merger is the way to go with or without organizational support or input. This decision may or may not make financial sense, but on an emotional level, the deal is going to close no matter what. For our example, let's say that one family grew and prospered on the east coast of the United States and the other in Vietnam. Here are some of the surface integration issues:

- The location of the new "headquarters"
- The disposition of one or both sources of income
- What to do with duplicate infrastructure such as real estate
- Continuity of education for the children
- Funding for the transition period

These items may be difficult, but they are pale in comparison to the people issues, such as

- Friends and social networks
- Proximity to family
- Customs, practices, and rituals (aka culture)
- Expectations of what the future will bring
- Disconnection from the decision to merge

The integration issues in families of meals, meal times, dress codes, curfews, acceptable language, decor, family events, television rules, Internet rules, friends, car usage, and so on run parallel to artifacts of company culture such as social networks, policies, procedures, processes, friendships, identification with the brand, and so on. What we can count on is that free radicals will form in families and in organizations during mergers. We can further count on people not only thinking that their "cheese has been moved" but in many cases they will sense that their cheese has been melted. Whether we are talking about a blended family or a blended business model, several things are common to the path moving forward:

- The "executives" must be unified on a clear plan on how the merger will take place.

- People in the organization must be engaged in the planning.
- Free radicals must be dealt with so that they do not derail the change.
- People need to be given things to do to engage them in the change.
- Lines of communication must be open and used extensively to manage expectations.

We have seen the best results relative to this set of challenges when a balanced set of executives have followed a general path such as:

- Use a team of people representing a broad cross-section of the business to create the integration plan, including organizational structure, go-to-market strategy, branding strategy, and communication plan
- Launch activities to join the two organizations in constructive dialogue to create social connections
- Take fast action to fill roles, which keeps ambiguity to a minimum and reduces the time between announcement and action
- Execute consistent messaging throughout all levels of the organization

Mergers are difficult and messy. By not expecting the process to be clean and tidy, it is possible to embrace the mess as a normal course of moving forward and to make sure that no expectation is created that it will be clean and painless. This is why it becomes critical to have HR engaged as a strategic partner and that spin be kept to a minimum. Mergers put leadership skills to the test, disrupt that which made the company successful in the past, and test the ability to articulate clear strategy. Thinking about mergers in a different way—such as that of a blended family—can uncover significant opportunities to improve the integration effort.

Summary

Mergers are about the acquisition of people. In the rare instance that there is a merger of industrial processes, perhaps this is less the case. For the most part, however, mergers are more and more a matter of the acquisition of talent, which is not hardwired into factory processes and machinery. The mentality appropriate for the acquisition of one steel mill by another in order to gain economy of scale is not applicable when the assets of the enterprise are largely intellectual property embedded in the minds of people. One of the best ways to increase the odds of success in mergers is to set the balance sheets, income statements, and hard asset lists aside and focus on how you are going to integrate the people. This is an unnatural act for the numerically driven analytical mind. It is also an unnatural act for the highly competitive, impatient, hard-driving extroverts who rush the processes of mergers, missing the opportunity to go a little slower in the beginning in order to gain speed overall.

When companies merge, powerful basic ingredients that allow transformation are created. People get pushed out of their comfort zones. It is the opening to create a new identity and vision. Anxiety is a natural ingredient of being outside the comfort zone and inside the process of creating a new vision. People who cannot make the change must be allowed to find the next best alternative for them; otherwise, they become a drain on the system and prevent progress. By creating teams composed of people representing both entities, assigning clear objectives, and holding accountability for results, you set the stage for culture transformation and a natural selection process for those who cannot make the change.

Ten Key Questions

1. Do you acknowledge for yourself and others that people are central to the business model?

2. Do you understand the range of emotions present during a merger or acquisition?

3. Do you have the capability for helping people move on or move out?

4. Do you have a plan for the free radicals who will pop up?

5. Do you have a vision, strategy, and business plan that all new teams can rally around?

6. Does your integration plan call for moving fast?

7. Do you have a communication strategy and plan?

8. Have you done any social network analysis to understand where the central actors are in the organization?

9. Does the integration plan deal with people issues as a first priority?

10. Have specific work packages and teams been created to accomplish specific goals postintegration?

11

SPIN IS OVERRATED
FOR CREATING VALUE

I did not have sexual relations with that woman.
—*Bill Clinton, January 26, 1998*

Two prisoners sat in a murky prison awaiting their fate. They had both been convicted of crimes against the kingdom and were sentenced to death. Their final chance for appeal came when the king visited them in prison and asked each one in turn whether he had any final words to say on his behalf.

The king turned to the first prisoner, who replied by saying that although he had committed the crimes of which he was accused, he was generally a good person, and that if the king would grant him a pardon, he would remain a loyal subject for the remainder of his life. The king simply replied, "Appeal denied," and told the man to expect his execution the following day.

The king turned to the second prisoner, who asked the king if he owned a horse. The king replied that he owned many horses. The prisoner told him that if granted a year, he would teach one of the king's horses to sing. The king looked amazed, and after a short argument as to the validity of the claim, the king accepted the offer and postponed the execution.

After the king and his guards left the dungeon, the first prisoner turned to the second and said, "You know that you can't do any such thing. I've known you all your life, and you've never done anything of the sort." The second prisoner simply replied, "What you say is true, but on the other hand, I just bought myself a year, and in that time many things could happen: the king could die, the horse could die, or I could actually figure out how to do it."

This is an example of what we have come to know as spin. The so-called spin doctor is the person who finds some way to obscure, shift attention, reframe, or otherwise reduce the heat of a situation. Manipulating facts into factoids, creating disinformation, and outright counterclaiming are all part of the standard practice of spinning.

The experiences with Enron, WorldCom, Tyco, and Bernie Madoff make the economic wreckage of spin relatively obvious. In organizations like these, spin is a pastime or a sport, but in many others, it is used as a central element of communication. When an organization is working toward transforming itself from one business model to another, communication and trust are critical, and time is of the essence. There is more than enough difficulty in transforming organizations without the decreased trust, added confusion, and crippling delay that result from spin.

Luckily, spin is easily seen and can be eradicated. Given the right leadership, spin can be replaced with candor that delivers benefit to the organization.

Candor—the Antidote for *Caveat Emptor*

The expression *Caveat emptor* translates as "Let the buyer beware," and serves as a general warning to buyers to beware of claims made. Spin is not new. Human beings have been engaging in it nonstop for centuries. For example, consider the spin normally involved in the sale of a company. In a typical case, the seller of the company would do everything he could to avoid discussing the company's skeletons in the closet. Everyone knows they exist, but they are rarely talked about. This results in a negotiation based on assumptions, not facts—in other words, a crock. If we take the spin approach, the seller is hoping that the buyer will underestimate the skeletons and that she will extract "premium value." But because the buyer assumes the seller is "spinning" the sale, she may overestimate the number of skeletons in the closet to protect her risk. In the end, the only question is about who gets to hold the bag on the error in valuation. Evidently, because more than two-thirds of acquisitions fail to deliver real value to the shareholders, the spin doctors on the sales side are currently winning two out of three bullshit-slinging contests.

Now consider the same situation, but using a candid approach. We will call the company for sale ZipCo. ZipCo was solvent, growing, and financially secure. It had a strong product line that was expanding and innovative. Several billion dollars were on the line. Investment bankers were called in. Lawyers and accountants had done all the due diligence needed. Meeting after meeting took place with prospective buyers, where the case was presented for the sale of the company. This is usually where the spin gets thick, but in the case of selling this particular company, an entirely different approach was taken. Whereas it is normally not thought to be a great idea to expose the problems and shortcomings of a company, the management team of ZipCo took a more candid approach and outlined shortcomings in market penetration, product line enhancement, skill development, systems capability, and so on. The investment bankers accused the management team of blowing the deal, but just the opposite was true. By hearing disclosure of the places where ZipCo was challenged along with its strong points, the buyers had more confidence in the real value of the company, which made them more interested in the deal, not less. And this makes sense, doesn't it? Anyone who has a background in business knows that businesses are never perfect. All business models have a few warts. There are always problems in execution, some unhappy customers, some gaps in capability and capacity. A prospective buyer knows this, and every seller knows where those weaknesses lie.

In the case of ZipCo, the price paid was at a strong multiple of earnings, and the value of the company postacquisition remained high. Candor in the process of executing the acquisition was cited as a major element in making the deal easier and more attractive. Spin would have hurt the deal.

As a second example, consider the approach taken by a project team that needed to tell a customer that the team was behind on delivering a project. The company, which we will call PlusCo, was new and had emerging technology that showed great promise. However, one of PlusCo's teams was behind schedule on a high-profile customer project and knew that the clients would be disappointed. A meeting with really high profile clients when the story is not what the clients want to hear is a fertile area for spin to start, and in fact the team held meetings with the express agenda of creating spin. When the leadership team heard how this team was going to spin their situation, they coached the team to reduce the status report to the facts at hand, tell the whole story about where the project stood, and provide the clients a realistic set of expectations moving forward. When the team took this candid approach, the clients' response was anything but what the team expected. The clients expressed disappointment in the progress, but satisfaction in being told the truth. They also told the team that they basically knew where the project stood, and had the PlusCo team lied or spun the story, PlusCo would have probably lost the project and, if not, certainly future projects.

The simple truth is that people are becoming increasingly fatigued by the amount of spin they are asked to sort through and digest as a result of spin. Seems that a little honesty and candor go a long way, and all the effort to cover up, soft-pedal, and conceal is largely wasted. In transforming organizations, there is no time to waste on decoding the spin and unraveling convoluted stories and excuses. It turns out that the fastest and least-effort thing to do is also the most honest.

Recognize the Symptoms

Spin can be readily detected in most cases, but is subtle in others. Learning to spot the spin and put a stop to it benefits the organization by increasing the outright honesty in communication. The following are distinctions and ways we have found useful in dealing with spin.

Factoids Versus Facts

A factoid is an emphatic statement declared as if it were true, but is really more of a supposition, hypothesis, or wishful thinking. In a *60 Minutes* broadcast in early March 2009, Bernard Madoff is shown telling a group of investors that it is "virtually impossible" to violate rules of trading without being detected. As we later found out, it *was* possible, but Madoff seemed believable because the reality was harder to believe. The reality was that for two decades, Madoff perpetrated the biggest fraud in history. Here is how spin works, though. Suppose Madoff were put on the witness stand and confronted with the statement he made of "virtual impossibility." He could argue that he probably was detected, but that he simply was never called on his scheme. Unfortunately, from a logic point of view, there is no way to prove the nonexistence of anything. Existence can be proven; nonexistence cannot. The statement of "virtual impossibility" is a factoid. It is not a fact, but was stated as one.

There are two things to note about the use of factoids. First, a factoid has the advantage of superficial validity. At first glance, Madoff is making a statement as if it were fact, and on the surface, it seems as if it could be true. Second and closely related, factoids have a tough time standing up to a request for evidence. Think of how hard it would be to prove the "virtual impossibility" of going without detection. One would have to set up repeated scams and be continuously caught. So statements made to declare the nonexistence of something without at least anecdotal evidence are likely to be factoids. Some factoids that are dangerous in organizational transformation concern any or all of the following subjects and terms:

- "Strategic" accounts
- "Mission critical"
- "Sustainability"
- "Disruptive"
- "Scalable"
- "Best practice"
- "High performance"

Bending the Truth out of Shape

A second form of spin is the intentional distortion of the truth. The most minor form of this is résumé fluffing. If a person worked in various countries and got fired from the company due to lack of performance, she can translate this as "international experience" on her résumé. She did work abroad, but casting it as "international experience" is somewhat disingenuous, as she was fired for her lack of performance. A more deadly example of distortion of the truth was the claim that there were weapons of mass destruction in Iraq. The facts and factoids flew, and bending of the truth was in high gear, as evidenced by the later failure to find any WMDs in Iraq. As a result, the effort on the part of the press, the military, and the government to discover what was known, how it was known, what information was factual versus anecdotal, and what sources were used has been massive.

With regard to organizations, it is likely that the truth will get bent out of shape when it comes to a company's market share, the size of the market, merger synergies, acquisition value, and cost estimates. Although nobody's information is perfect, there is clearly improvement to be made in the providing of information.

Proof by Repeated Assertion

People often become convinced of their own flawed logic simply by repeating it enough. Witness the executive mantra. Mantras are formed by repeating a factoid, a spurious fact, or an outright fabrication often enough that it starts to gain traction in the company dialogue. One example is the repeated assertion, promulgated by many organizations, of being both a product producer and solution source. When an organization attempts both products and systems, it is a bit like trying to get one organization brain to do two things simultaneously. The cartoon strip "Dilbert" featured a new employee named Amber Dextrous who had her brain severed in half so that she could multitask. In the cartoon, Amber unfortunately drowns while attempting to drink water and talk simultaneously. This is similar to our experience in working with organizations that try to be product producers and solution providers simultaneously. In the absence of any proof that this form of being ambidextrous is a possibility (actually there is more evidence to the contrary), executives have attempted to create proof by repeating the assertion that going for ambidexterity is the key to success. The test for this symptom is simple. If the roots of the assertions being made come from a person who makes an unfounded claim and then begins to refer to the number of times claimed as proof of validity, spin is in full swing.

Brilliant but Cruel

An old saying goes something to the effect that if you cannot dazzle them with brilliance, baffle them with bullshit. That is the essence of brilliant but cruel. When people have large amounts of information, high intellectual capability, and fast processing speed, they are perfect candidates for being brilliant but cruel. This involves driving points home in a fast barrage of facts, factoids, repeated assertions, and outright guesses all rolled up in a nonstop fire-hose delivery. Some of these factoids and assertions take the form of criticisms, negative messages, and intimidating comments, which serve to drain those around them so that no one has the desire or energy to challenge the points. It has been said that a good test of leadership is to measure the amount of energy people take away from a conversation with another person. Brilliant but cruel people leave an empty shell on the ground after a conversation because they suck the life out of the people around them.

Understand the Damage

JR was a manager in the company for a decade and had operated various parts of the business globally with great success. His former employer regularly hired him back as a consultant. But JR indicated that one of the last things he would ever consider would be the reentry into any large company. When asked why, he said that he simply could not stand the idea of people coming to work and spending time attending meetings in which they lie to each other about what is really going on. JR had the wherewithal to leave the company environment. The people who do not leave, but face companies with enormous amounts of spin, are paying the price for spin with a lack of trust, lowered morale, and confusion.

Lack of Trust

People have a well-developed sense of spin. We probably all know when it is going on. When someone gets caught in the spin cycle, trust is the first casualty. Checking the validity of every single assertion is not practical. But when it turns out that the compensation plan is not quite what it was supposed to be, or when the synergies that the deal was predicated upon come to light as products of a spin cycle, the recovery of trust may not be within reach. Apologies don't really cut it. When the photo of Michael Phelps smoking a controlled substance made the front pages of magazines and television newscasts, apologies did not put the endorsements back in place, nor did they repair the reputation damage. Bernard Madoff will never recover his reputation. Leaders must understand the risks of loss of trust when they are engaging in spin. Organizational transformation is a time of extreme change. People are strained to make changes amid doing their "day job." Lack of trust makes transformation all the more difficult.

Lowered Morale, Motivation, and Energy

People are not designed to work at a high level of morale, motivation, and energy inside a fundamentally dishonest structure. Once the WMDs don't show up, whether that is metaphorically the market, the product, the earnings, the compensation, or some other spin factor, the deflation of the organization is almost physically visible. Not every spin cycle is as enormous as Bernard Madoff's or Kenneth Lay's or Richard Nixon's. Most of what we are talking about here are the day-to-day transactions that seem benign in the moment. After all, what is the difference between exaggeration and spin? If someone attempts to use hyperbole to declare that the company is going to become "indispensable" to its clients, people can feel the discord when they know that is not going to happen. This discord demands the expenditure of mental energy to sort out what was said into believable and unbelievable categories. The harder people have to work to separate fact from fiction, the less energy they have for doing something productive. It is hard to know what the real cost of spin might be in organizations, but suffice it to say, it is not free.

Confusion

Every time a president speaks, the pundits spend hours dissecting and analyzing parts of the speech. Various interpretations circulate as to what was said, what was meant, and what it all means. The same happens with executive conversations. After some meetings, people spend time trying to figure out what was said, what was meant, and what in the world to do about it. Spin aggravates this problem. The greater the spin, the greater the confusion. What is worse is that it seems that executives who create spin encourage people to adopt the same practice. What we end up with is spinners of spin.

Lead by Example

In our experience, the amount of spin in an organization is a function of the attitude of the leadership. Leaders must examine their role in creating an environment that encourages spin. Some leaders were groomed by spinners themselves, so they may not even know that they are engaging in spin. Others are aware of what they're doing, but continue to get away with it for years. Spin can be a career-enhancing move right up until it creates a career nosedive. There are a few things leadership can do to reduce or eliminate use of spin in the organization.

Conduct Spin-Free Meetings

We suggest that you declare your meetings to be spin-free zones. When the agenda or the presentations are beginning to spin out of control, the facilitator must bring the discussion back to the relevant information. It is possible that spin in a meeting is used as a cover-up for information a person does not want to disclose. It is also possible that it is a cover for incompetence. In either case, if the spin cannot be controlled to the point of getting the discussion back on track, consideration should be given to taking the item offline. You can also create ground rules to guide meeting quality, and discuss spin as an effect of a poor meeting. When someone is slinging factoids, repeatedly asserting factoids, or being brilliant but cruel, the facilitator can guide him back to the rules of engagement.

Deliver Effective Feedback

Whether spin is occurring in a meeting or one-on-one, it is likely to stop only by your providing feedback in a constructive way, be it to a colleague or to your boss. Feedback about spin can be difficult to give effectively without putting the spinner in a defensive position. For the most part, when you are confronting spin, the object is to put no spin on the feedback. So when giving the feedback to a spinner, you are best off if you confine the feedback to the observable. For example, a person might say that the reason the company should take a deal with a prospective client at a drastically reduced price, even if it creates losses for the company, is that the customer is a strategic account. "Strategic account" is a factoid until it is proven by facts. Taking a confrontational approach, you would ask, "When did losing money on sales become strategic?" Taking a constructive approach, you would ask the presenter for a clearer definition of "strategic account"—how and why this client is a strategic account and what is its long-term value. The feedback for spinners should encourage their return to facts from factoids, repeated assertions, and brilliant but cruel antics.

Improve Coaching to Teams

Teams get into the spin cycle when attempting to package bad news. But bad news is bad only because of the judgment laid on the facts. The facts are just a statement of where things stand. Every interpretation of the fact is a judgment. The Dow Jones average at the close of every day is a fact. But the interpretation of the average is where the spin starts. If you lost all your money in Bernard Madoff's Ponzi scheme, the economic situation is definitely not what you wanted and is therefore a "bad thing" from that perspective. If you pulled all your money out of the stock market and put it in gold, it is not nearly so bad, because the rest of the world just went on sale. When a team of people is considering how to package bad news, the leader needs to coach them to suspend judgment until the information is gathered, assembled, and understood from a factual perspective.

Now for the really big news: feelings are facts too. There are a limited number of types of feelings: mad, sad, glad, and scared. As we all know, there are infinite variations of these, but social science basically boils them down to good old-fashioned anger, depression, happiness, and fear. And because your team members have these feelings, your challenge as a coach is to figure out which of these feelings is running the dialogue and how to keep that feeling from causing the team to do something damaging. When you coach teams, reading the underlying emotion and guiding the team to prepare their actions based on a factual frame will help them create new alternatives, gather relevant information, think in an improved way, get clear on their values, and then take appropriate action.

In the famous example of Bill Clinton and Monica Lewinsky, we can see how his use of righteous indignation spun out of control and ended up in testimony that centered around the definition of the word *is*. In coaching teams, the idea is to end the spin before it builds momentum. The problem with not telling the truth is having to remember too many things and to keep track of what lie was told to whom. The same applies to spin— it actually causes us to create plausible deniability because we subconsciously know that we have to have a back door to escape the embedded lie. The truth is simply much easier.

Think Long Term

It is easy to get caught in the trap of short-term thinking. Part of the spin problem comes from saying and doing things that have no immediate impact but create a long-term liability. There is a lag in time between when we do or say something and when the repercussions are likely to occur. This lag creates a temptation to do or say something that works for the short term but not for the long term. The following are some ways we have found to be effective in reducing the temptation to spin by considering longer-term impacts.

Use the "Front Page Test"

In the end, when spin becomes front-page news, there is much to be lost in terms of trust and credibility. But not all spin ends up as front-page tabloid material; in fact, some of the cost of spin never surfaces in a tangible way. One way to curb the tendency to spin is to think of each person as having a front page in her mind. When spin is exposed or detected, it creates a "headline" that affects her prevailing organizational view of what is real, what is phony, whom to trust, and ultimately how to decide. So when you are communicating, it is critical that you give your communication the front page test—in other words, consider what the ultimate truth is going to look like when it makes the headlines, whether actual or metaphorical.

Test for "Quarterly Results" Bias

When giving quarterly results and guidance, executives enter a unique spin zone. Much has been written and lamented about how a quarterly focus is detrimental to the long-term health of the organization. If the way results are delivered gives any opening to create negative spin, the company suffers. If the results are overplayed, the company suffers. The question of what is "just right" is a tricky one because "just right" may not exist.

You need to communicate to the market so that you do not spin the quarterly result to the long-term detriment of the business. Releasing information that makes the quarterly result look better at the expense of long-term performance is to be avoided. Businesses have a life cycle of indefinite length. Focusing on the short-term value of quarterly result performance can shorten the life cycle. Just look at the case of Enron.

Aggressively Eradicate Spin Sources

There probably is no greater task of leadership than the eradication of spin sources. Spin can spread through an organization like cancer. Through coaching and feedback, some of the spreaders of factoids, the brilliant but cruel, and the repeated assertion experts can help contribute to a healthy organization, but some cannot. Your goal is to locate and improve or eradicate spinners in the organization. If the spin cycle is not stopped, it is a failure of leadership.

Not surprisingly, leaders are guilty of spin as well. In fact, the first person to break the habit may even be the leader. Consider the following story about Gandhi.

A woman came to Gandhi one day to ask that her child be told to stop eating so much sugar. Gandhi replied that he wanted the woman to bring her child back in two weeks. In two weeks, the woman brought her child back, at which time Gandhi reportedly told the child to reduce the amount of sugar the child was consuming. The woman asked Gandhi why he could not have told the child that two weeks prior. Gandhi replied that two weeks prior, he himself was consuming too much sugar.

Without being first to break the habit, you put yourself in a "Do as I say, not as I do" situation. Any attempt to lead a change without the leader being the first to change is a source of cynicism because it is a demonstration of hypocrisy.

Summary

Whether looked at macroscopically or microscopically, spin is overrated for creating value at any level of the enterprise. The addition of spin and the suppression of candor are relatively widespread, degrading value in the long run by overinflation in the short run. By understanding its roots in the normal course of human interaction, you become able to lead by example, provide feedback, and coach yourself and your teams to a higher level of candor and a lower level of damaging spin.

Ten Key Questions

1. How much nonproductive rhetoric gets slung at your meetings?

2. Do you take steps to stop people from bending the truth?

3. Are people in the organization attempting to prove their point by repeated assertion alone?

4. Are brilliant but cruel people destroying teamwork in your organization?

5. How much trust in your team is being lost through spin?

6. Is spin a factor in reducing morale for your people?

7. Is spin causing confusion and inefficiency in your organization?

8. Are you ready to lead by example in reducing spin?

9. Do you make sure that communications would make good front-page copy?

10. Have you eliminated the bias caused by a focus on quarterly results?

12

CONSULTANTS ARE NOT AN EXCUSE FOR NOT KNOWING YOUR BUSINESS

> Customer: "Sounds good, let's do it. When can we begin?"
>
> Consultant: "We are more like idea people; we are not practitioners."

After weeks of effort by a small army of bright young consultants working with the client based on their "statement of work" (SOW), the moment has come. The data are in. The analysis is complete. The slide deck has been created. In a very professional fashion, the consultant provides the context, lays out the agenda, and begins the presentation. The slides begin with the background for the analysis. This is followed by the listing of the processes by which the data were gathered using a cross-functional team in close collaboration with all stakeholders. Chart after chart is shown, and all the latest animation techniques have been used to increase the impact of the graphic displays. Last to be presented is the conclusion: What accounts for the difference in sales performance across sales regions? The conclusion: sales are not correlated with

1. Salesperson's process for managing the sales pipeline
2. Salesperson's time in position
3. Customer types

4. Customer sizes

5. Any of fifteen other attributes

So what does account for the difference? No clue. After an hour of data presentation, the consultant has summarized everything that the customer already knew, provided no new insight, and recommended no path forward to finding a solution to the customer's problem.

In another conference room halfway around the globe, a slide deck is showing how the revenue from current sales does not match development expenditures on future products. Although this information is accurate, the question is, "So what?" Development spending is about future revenue, not current revenue. They are not *supposed* to match. The consultant replies that more analysis will be required to uncover the significance. More money needs to be placed in the SOW in order to gain further "insight."

These scenarios and thousands like them are played out daily in the world of professional services. For the most part, consultants and clients are in a mutual love-hate relationship. Consultants have their jokes; corporate insiders have theirs. Scott Adams, the creator of "Dilbert," probably makes the most money of all the players in the never-ending game between companies and their hired advisers.

What is hard to find is practical information about what to do to create a value-added relationship between consultant and client. The subject does not come up very often in business literature. It could be that neither the company nor the consultant has much incentive to be candid about its views of the other party. It might be a problem of too much dirty laundry on both sides, and nobody really wants to see that much underwear. In this chapter, we will endeavor to create a balanced view of the situation as we have experienced it and provide a framework for improving a system that needs a drastic upgrade.

Today's Common Consulting Model

Having engaged dozens of consultants over time, we will start by looking at the consulting model we are most familiar with. In stepping back and examining the underpinning logic of the consulting model, we see a few common behaviors.

Do a Massive (Looking) Amount of Research

Consulting companies spend large sums of money generating huge amounts of information in studies that attempt to show connection between certain variables and certain outcomes. Jim Collins, who wrote the books *Built to Last* and, more recently, *Good to Great,* is a good example of a research-oriented consultant. The implication of his research is that what made a difference to the companies he studied has significance to you. As with Tom Peters's *In Search of Excellence,* this research is sometimes well designed and is sometimes part real, part urban legend, part pure wishful thinking. No matter the type, it all looks great in the charts and graphs. The following outlines how the research is monetized within a typical consulting model.

Bake Up a Fresh Batch of Best Practices

The challenge for the consultant here is to find the pattern inside the research that has general applicability and convince the potential client that implementation of "best practices" is the ticket to a bright future. Armed with all this research, the consulting firm can now frame any problem in such a manner that it just happens to have the solution to it. Four thousand slides later, after hearing a presentation usually designed to inform the client about how much of a problem it has and sell the next phase of services, the company agrees that if the solution worked for GE or Cisco or Google, then it will work for the company also. Even when the difference between correlation and causation is plainly in view, the pitch seems so credible that signing up for the same thing that made Jack Welch successful is too tempting to pass up. With the sale made, it is time for the team to arrive on-site.

Send in a Senior Partner and a Bunch of Fresh MBAs

This is where the real money begins to be made. Agree on a price for services. Begin billing at once. Soon the client company will feel as if it is making car loan payments. It hates to pay each month, but if it wants to get to where it is going, the company must pay the loan.

Consulting firms are no different from any other company; they are in business to make money. For many consultants, it is a good day when the phone rings and it's a company that cannot fully describe the problem and cannot articulate what it believes it needs or even wants. What the company does know is that it needs a consultant to help.

Lay Out the Three-Phase Plan

Consulting companies come in and lay out their plan in three phases (usually). Phase one involves researching the problem. They must conduct multiple interviews to make sure they have a correct view of the organization. Research on the business model must be done to ensure that they have the correct understanding of what the company is trying to do. As part of the process, they must connect with some customers to be certain that they have the end users' perspective on the organization. This stage will take three to six weeks of work, along with fees and expenses to get the information required by the consultant to move to the next phase. Phase two is the framing of the problem. Not coincidentally, the framing of the problem exactly matches the models generated in the original research. Great news—because phase three is the two-year engagement to implement the solution.

Arm the Account Team with the Latest Set of Slides That Will Provide an Off-the-Shelf Solution

Tools and templates are very useful. So useful, in fact, that a consulting company can do the research and boil it down to templates that can be used for data gathering and presentations. All that is needed is the same stuff that was collected on the last account to be populated into the templates.

Customize the Solution, If Possible, and Charge More for Some Tweaking of the Slides

Mostly, the so-called customization translates into adding headers, footers, and cover pages, but there might be an occasional data field or table cell that needs to be modified. The best way for consulting companies to make maximum profit is to use standardized materials that deal with common problems with prefabricated solutions that are preformatted into presentations. This approach creates a number of economies for the consultant but does not necessarily generate specific benefit to the client where it has unique needs.

Create Ongoing Dependency

Now the consulting firm is in the driver's seat. It has the account exactly where it wants it to be. The final step is to create an ongoing dependency for its services for not only current but also future problems. This is not always easy, but if the consultant can pull it off, the account can become a cash cow. It is a great model, and it works. It works more often for the consultant than it does for the company, but both parties get something out of it.

And Your Point Is...?

If you are a consultant, you may be wondering what the problem is. After all, this model has been used successfully for decades and has made a lot of money for a lot of people. If you are a consumer of professional services, however, you may be wondering if there is a better way. Our intention here is not to slam consulting firms; they are in business to make money based on the value they create, and many of them deliver on this requirement very well. The challenge we raise is whether consulting firms and the companies that engage them could be making better use of their time and money. Consulting is a multibillion-dollar industry. But if it's so invaluable, why is it one of the first things eliminated in a downturn (after morning donuts and travel expenses)? If the consulting trade is so valuable, why is it considered so discretionary? If the company can do without the consulting support in a downturn, was it really necessary in the first place? In 2006, Stan Abraham and Robert J. Allio wrote an article titled "The Troubled Strategic-Business-Advice Industry: Why It's Failing Decision Makers" (*Strategy & Leadership* 34, no. 3: 4–13). In the article, the authors lay out the fundamental structural issues that exist for companies, consulting practices, higher education, publishers, and researchers, and cite problems with the business model of consulting. Some of the problems with the business model stem from the fact that consultants' compensation is not linked to company risk or performance, there is insufficient knowledge transfer to the client, and consulting firms don't evolve the effectiveness of their consulting model. We have found some of the same things to be true in our experience. In addition, we would add the following:

- The cycle of using research to imply that there are common solutions that can be directly applied to transformation in all companies is based on flawed logic.
- Most of the fresh minds that show up in a consulting engagement have never solved a real business problem in their young lives.
- There is a huge amount of waste in the process of getting to the real issues in the organization.

- Consulting solutions are usually long on advice and short on execution.
- The organization is not engaged to do the heavy lifting, which means that it builds no capability.

What the Consultant Model Should Be

In order to create a better relationship between consultant and client, there needs to be a better way of approaching the client engagement. Transformation is about the orchestration of multiple disciplines. Consultants seem to enter into the client relationship in accordance with Maslow's fundamental attribution error: those who are good with hammers tend to think of everything as a nail. If this is the case, the door is open to preconceived notions about the client's problem and can result in predesigned solutions. As noted in *Executing Your Strategy*, the leaders of Motorola created the Iridium solution and then went and tried to find a problem and market for it to serve. Consultants do this with services. The data come first, then the model, then the search for a customer to help with it. This approach does not work when professional services are needed to help with transformation. The need in transformation is to find ways to integrate various disciplines in unique ways.

Following are some of the changes to the consulting model we'd suggest in order to meet the needs of organizations undergoing transformation.

Don't Get High on Your Own Supply

Consultants need to get better at organizational diagnostics. Research is great, but as several authors have pointed out (Christensen and Rosenzweig, for instance), by the time a best practice is researched, peer-reviewed, documented, implemented in several places, baked into best practices, and written up and made ready for market, it is not only old but also only applicable to the specific situation under study. The lead time for publishing a book is over a year, and the book is written at the end of the research cycle. The world moves too fast and the needs of customers are too variable to use the one-size-fits-all approach. Consultants need flexible frameworks and adaptable tools. Overreliance on research-based approaches has a limit that is often overreached in the search for a new nail to hit with the hammer the consultant has created.

Know How to Use the Word "No"

Most consultants can tell you that the one thing that permeates the executive suite is the inability to say no. In some cases, this is what spawns the need for the consultant: the organization is overloaded with too much work to be able to complete any of it successfully. The same goes for the consultant. There are places where the consultant should be and places where he should not. If the consultant literally has no background in the problem at hand, he must refer the client elsewhere even when that means less work for him. This problem pervades every business from the mom-and-pop automotive repair facility to the high-profile consultancies of the world. Knowing when to say no is a skill and an underdeveloped one at that. Consultants need a preengagement screening process that keeps them from getting into areas where they are unlikely to generate value.

Improve the Agreement Structure

Some consultants create solid agreements with their clients, and some do not. Rarely do the agreements specify what to do with the messy parts of the engagement. This is a mistake for companies engaged in transformation, where massive changes will occur in some parts of the organization and individuals are going to have more than their cheese moved. In the structure of the consulting agreement, it is important that there be a way to deal with the inevitable antibody reaction to any real change taking place. As soon as a consultant touches a really important element that needs to be changed, the company's immune system will try to surround and expel the intruding consultant. The governance of the engagement must take this into account so that the client can directly address the situation and a decision can be made as to how the engagement will proceed. In all probability, the person at the source of the real organizational issue is going to lead the charge. If this person is highly powerful and there is no previously agreed-on process for dealing with his or her allergic reaction to change, the engagement can be rendered useless. When this happens, it ruins the momentum of the engagement, loses the consultant a referral, and hardens the organization to change. Clear agreement on issue resolution, escalation, and decision making is critical to changing this dynamic.

Establish Clear Accountability

The old joke about how consultants are people who charge you for telling you what you already know makes some interesting points. First of all, if organizations already know what consultants tell them, why did the recommended actions remain undone? And if organizations know that consultants are going to tell them what they already know, why do they enter agreements that ensure this outcome?

We suggest that consultants tie their compensation to company results where possible. In practice, this means that once the consultant prescribes something implementable, the company follows through on it, and the results are attributable to what the consultant recommended. Beyond the problem of establishing whether the successful results are caused by or simply correlated with the consultant's advice, this arrangement requires a clear agreement between the client and consultant. If the consultant is going to enter into a performance-based contract, then the company must sign up for the implementation. Mutual accountability is an absolute must. Both sides are accountable for actions and results.

What if results aren't visible for a long period of time and have a long gestation period? This is what makes the value of consulting hard to pin down and even harder to prove. The best that can be done is to specify as clearly as possible what quid pro quo the engagement is based on.

Decide Whether You Want a Fish or the Capability to Fish

There is a marked difference between management consulting and other professional services. If you go to a lawyer for a contract to be written, it is unlikely that the lawyer is going to tell you how to create the contract for yourself. If you get a haircut, your knowledge of haircutting is not part of the deal. Tax preparers do not train you on tax preparation as part of doing a tax return for you. But in the case of management consulting, companies expect a transfer of knowledge from the consultant, and often complain, "We could have done that for ourselves." This latter point may be true, but the fact is that they did not do so. Further, just because they received the service does not entitle them to the underpinning process knowledge, unless the agreement specifically says so. And that is the point. The consulting model must include a specific declaration of whether knowledge transfer is in or out of scope. If it is in scope, work and costs are different than if it is not. The question of knowledge transfer must not be left to assumption.

Specify Who Is Doing the Heavy Lifting

One approach to generating organizational capability is to let the organization do the heavy lifting of data gathering, number crunching, analysis, and so on. Some clients are best served by letting them struggle with the heavy-lifting portion, which will build up their long-term capability. If the reason for the consulting engagement is that the organization does not have these capabilities, this is a moot point, but in many cases, the organization has the bandwidth and is just missing the direction. Although this approach may cut down the size of the engagement, increase interface complexity, and cause internal prioritization issues, among other things, it is a viable way for customers to contain costs and gain long-term benefits. The consulting model is improved by having the customer choose whether or not to take on the time-consuming work of slogging through the process.

Hand a Microphone to the Voice in the Wilderness

We have all worked in organizations where we have seen consultants come in, implement some changes that were already widely known to be needed, and watch the leadership congratulate themselves on having killed the dragon. Some consultants assume that clients do not know how to solve their own problems. We are of a different opinion. The organizations we have worked with have people who are well versed in their problems and know what to do about them. What they don't have is a means of giving their ideas a voice that can be heard and acted on. They feel like voices in the wilderness, yelling at the top of their lungs but not being heard. So they remain silent. But if their voices are listened to, the level of engagement from those people will rise dramatically. People have tremendous amounts of tacit knowledge about their organization and how things really happen that no consultant is ever going to reach. Bringing out these voices needs to be more the norm than the exception.

Know When Yes Becomes No

It seems like such a great thing at the time. The account looks like a good fit for the skills of the consultancy, the plan looks good, and the agreements are all in place. Then reality sets in. This engagement means the client will have to do some real work. But then other things come up—competitors change direction, the situation looks more difficult, setting priorities is a problem, meetings get missed, and so on. Stories and excuses as to why things are not happening start to flow like water. What started off right turns sour as the engagement comes off the rails.

This is crunch time for the consulting engagement. Rather than maximizing the consultant's income in the short run, the consulting model needs to contain exit criteria for circumstances in which it becomes clear that the engagement is not going to bear fruit. A "walk away" can be a good thing. It may be the wake-up call the client needs. Perhaps getting fired by the consultant will give the client pause for consideration. Perhaps not, but at least if the consultant exits, he or she preserves integrity. In this case, the person getting the severance package should be the consultant per the mutual accountability agreement mentioned earlier. Clients should never be allowed to weasel out of their accountability for follow-through. At least not for free.

Rationalize the Research

In the words of Abraham and Allio, "The people that have the time and motivation to do business research that could improve business processes are disconnected from those places and people that could benefit from their thinking." It seems that there might be some truth to the old statement,

Those who can ... do.
Those who cannot ... manage.
Those who cannot manage ... teach.
Those who cannot teach ... consult.
Those who cannot consult ... become researchers.

Cynical as it is, this string of roles does put researchers as far from the interface of getting things done as they can get. Consultants are only one step removed from researchers, reflecting the need to connect research with the reality of getting things done.

Consultancies need to align their research with the guidance they give their clientele. Too often consultants' advice strays from their own research. A case in point is the research done by a large consulting organization on the subject of mergers (D. Harding and S. Rovit, *Mastering the Merger*, Boston: Harvard Business School Press, 2004). There is nothing that brings up more transformational issues than mergers, so anything that can help better the miserable track record of mergers is welcome. By the authors' own estimates, only three in ten mergers deliver real value. In writing the book, the consulting firm conducted a survey on what tends to make mergers successful, which revealed the following:

1. Culture integration is addressed early on.
2. The best people are selected to lead the merged entity.
3. Integration is focused on value.
4. Leaders communicate extensively.

However, in writing their book, the consultants focused on a different set of themes:

1. Target deals according to a sound investment thesis.
2. Determine which deals to close and which to walk away from.
3. Prioritize which aspects of the businesses to integrate and which to leave independent.
4. Develop contingency plans for when deals inevitably go off track.

Did the authors read their own research? Is the book about what works or about what they wanted to talk about? The themes of the book advocate an approach that is anything but new and does not address the success factors indicated by the consultants' own research. Any research on how culture integration really works and how to select the team, create value, and promote leader communication would be greatly appreciated. However, the research and advice stay within the comfort zone of talking mostly about synergies, also known as places that can be cut.

Today's Common Company Model

When you pick up a business magazine or read any business book, you can count on a discussion about solving problems. It is true that most of what we do in a typical day is about solving problems. All of us believe that we can solve problems. From the time we get out of bed in the morning until we go to bed at night, we are solving problems and figuring out how to do things better or more efficiently. *How do I get around this traffic jam? How do I go to work and take care of the kids on this snow day? How do I make ends meet on this limited budget?* All of these are problems that we face and solve constantly. Then why is it that when we go to work and attempt to solve problems with our coworkers, we experience a limitless number of reasons why the group cannot get a problem solved?

A big reason for this has to do with needing to solve problems as a team, as opposed to solving problems independently. Every human being has her own innate way of thinking through problems that works for her. However, the challenge inside organizations is to create a process by which all these independent problem solvers can solve a range of problems together. Orchestrating transformation creates problems that the organization overall and the individuals in it have never solved before. It's not always a matter of the team not knowing the answer—sometimes they don't even know the question. In a struggle to get something positive to happen in the business, a company often falls into the following pattern:

- Reach the end of the rope

  This is the point when the organization realizes that the problem is something that cannot be solved at the level of current thinking in the organization.

- Engage a consultant to study the matter

  Through existing contacts, an expert is brought in to look the problem over and see what can be done.

- Define the problem

  Consultants review the issues and define the problem for (and sometimes with) the business.

- Experience death by PowerPoint

  Managers sit through hours of PowerPoint slides that summarize the consultants' findings.

- Think, *Sounds expensive—let's do it!*

  The management team signs a long-term high-cost engagement agreement to fix the problem.

- Go for low-hanging fruit

  The organization implements a portion of what is recommended.

- Change your mind

  Leaders eventually convince themselves that the changes are not really needed.

- Recognize that the problem is still not fixed

  Although there were lots of initiatives, the problem persists.

- Engage another consultant

  The organization restarts the process from the beginning.

The Should-Be Model for Companies

Transformation requires that you look at your business model differently. Patterns of thinking, problem-solving processes, group interaction, and team performance become embedded in corporate culture, which can become so powerful that any attempt to change it to another way of operation is almost impossible without third-party assistance. A detached and neutral third party may be the only way you can gain perspective on the situation, so the organization may end up using a consultant.

In any event, the tendency of a social network inside a company to resist change is well known. The entire leadership team is responsible for that culture and social network, and in many cases created them. It is next to impossible to adopt a different cultural approach with the same leadership, which is why, in many cases, executive replacement is required to effect change. To break with a pattern similar to the one we outlined in the preceding section, companies need to approach the situation differently.

Recognize That Transformation Is Different from Problem Solving

Problem solving occurs when a concise definition of a situation can be stated as a differential between what should be and what is. The focus is on understanding the deviation from the desired state, identifying the cause, and removing the cause. In contrast, transformation occurs when there is a recognition that what is working today is not going to work tomorrow. It is the differential between what is and what will be. It is not about things being out of line. It is about changing the line itself. Whereas problems are solved, transformation is *created*. Approaching transformation with a problem-solving mentality is like bringing a baseball bat to a tennis tournament. You will be able to hit the ball, but not in an effective fashion.

Beware the Old Business Model

Recognize that transformation is about fundamental change that poses major threats to major players who will use all their power and influence to protect systems within which they have done well in the past. As the future is created, people cling to the past. Recall how many people have been killed or maimed over the course of history for suggesting that the earth is not the center of the universe or that the world is not flat or for committing some other crime against existing mental models. A much less bloody but no less backstabbing model plays out in our organizations. Watch for who picks up the first knife. It is likely to be the people most threatened by change who are going to be the first to test the resolve of the change agent. They will create trouble, but not nearly as much as the ones who do their work silently and behind closed doors.

Get Ready, Willing, and Able

Recognize that no organization is ever ready for transformation on its own. Lack of readiness sometimes shows up as resistance to change on the basis of needing to lay all the groundwork first, as if leaders were creating a parallel universe that the organization can move to when everything is ready and proven. The first question is whether the organization sees a clear justification for change that indicates that it is ready. The second question is whether there is sufficient willpower (willingness) to sustain a change effort through the tough decisions that must be made. Third is the question of ability. There are a lot of people who would like to play golf at the level of Tiger Woods. The fact is that for 99.99 percent of the population (or more), that is simply out of the question. Organizations can talk all they want about reaching trusted adviser status as a solutions provider, but if that is truly out of range with regard to their current or attainable skill set, then transformation is merely a hallucination. Before engaging in a large-scale transformation, organizations should assess their readiness, willingness, and ability, so as to avoid a very expensive and frustrating experience. When engaging consultants, it is critical to know if they are going to help you with readiness, willingness, or ability, or some combination of the three.

Put Away the Can Opener

Before you engage in any transformational effort—with or without a consultant—recognize that it does not come in a can. The can that consultants want to sell you is largely dressed up as best practices. You would be more likely to make money by building a bonfire out of $100 bills than to engage in transformation off of some predesigned blueprint. In our experience, transformation involves seven layers of an organization. (We discuss this further in the Conclusion.) The way the layers are arranged and what is in each layer is different in every company. Although there are similarities and patterns, no two companies are alike, which means that there is no one best way to accomplish transformation. If someone shows up in your office with his formula "deck" for change, cancel the meeting and go for a walk. The walk will generate much more value.

Focus on Working on and Working to Transform

We are all so busy these days working in our businesses that we scarcely have time to think a coherent thought between e-mails, text messages, voice mails, and phone calls. The idea that we might devote some time to improving the business we are so busy working in is hard to implement because we are working 24/7 as it is. Adding another category of work to fundamentally transform the business might be the final straw if there is no room made for the effort. There is little sense in engaging a consultant if there is no time to support, listen, and act. That is why it is called an "engagement." It is about engaging the process via a consultant. Create some bandwidth and ensure that leaders understand the importance of working on and working to transform the business. If there is no bandwidth to work on and to transform the business, engaging a consultant in this space must account for the need for capacity as well as competency. Paying for analysis and advice you have no capacity to implement is a waste of money and of everyone's time.

Make a Good Draft Choice

Availability is not a skill set. This is true about putting together teams, and it is true about consultants. That consultants are available or recommended by a friend can be a harbinger of waste. Implement a screening process to select the right consultant to solve the company's problem. Make the selection using multiple viewpoints. Remember that if the decision is made by the people who are likely to need the most change, their input could be biased in favor of those who they think represent their interest the best.

In his book *Outliers* (New York: Little Brown, 2008), Malcolm Gladwell asserts that world-class expertise comes at about the ten-thousand-hour mark of experience. If you have no other way to screen candidates, check to see how far along the consultant is in putting in her ten thousand hours, and whether her expertise is what you need to effectively make the transformation in question. You'll place your best bet where you find the best match.

Know What You Want

Sounds simple enough. It is a little more challenging to accomplish, however. The main challenge in transformation is to know what you *do not* know. Blind spots are common. If someone does not understand the difference between a product sale and a consultative sale, or has no appreciation for the difference, it is unlikely that he will ask for consulting in that area. Transformation has the biggest "don't know what we don't know" problem of any type of change. The best defense for these blind spots is education. Make sure the organization is up on the latest thinking and information available on the subject so that when you engage a consultant, you can specify clearly what the company needs and what it does not need.

Provide Air Cover for Consultants on the Ground

Design the consultant's relationship with the company to provide access, sponsorship, and a way to tell the truth without getting neutralized by the organization. Figuring out what the real issues are and designing a transformation strategy and plan require end-to-end access to the organization. It is critical to let the organization know who the consultant is, why he is there, and what the scope of his involvement will be. This helps open the door for the consultant to get the information he needs. Once this is accomplished, it is critical that the consultant have a direct line to the sponsor in the organization to ask any and all questions. During the consultant's intelligence gathering, some people are likely to feel a bit threatened and begin the antibody process. The sponsor of the consulting engagement must be available to handle emerging conflicts. The consultant must also be given a forum for communication so that he can be candid about the problems the organization faces, without getting neutralized by the corporate antibodies. Consider giving the consultant the ability to provide feedback to the sponsor of the engagement via a customer scorecard rating the level of cooperation, communication, openness, collaboration, and so on that he has received from the people in the company.

Make a Conscious Choice About Building Organizational Capability

If the organization wants to gain knowledge transfer out of the consulting engagement, ensure that the consultant's contract includes the development of an employee who can provide the consulting service the next time the company needs this same work completed. This mentor-mentee relationship must be part of the services agreement up front. It is both unreasonable and unethical to send a person along to every session the consultant conducts to "take notes" with the intention of replicating what the consultant does. If you want the capability, you must contract for it, pay for it, and make it part of the deal. If you think that consultants cannot tell that they are being recorded, think again. It raises hell with trust in the relationship to know that the company is covertly "borrowing" the intellectual property that it took the consultant years to develop.

Calculate the Return on Consulting Up Front

Map out in defined terms what the return on consulting (ROC) will be. In the end, if a consultant fails to deliver a solution to a company's problem, the responsibility and the accountability should rest with the leadership of the company. Naturally, the consequence for the consultant is a failing business. From your company's point of view, factors that determine your ROC might include reduced costs, increased revenue, time savings, improved process efficiency, management time savings, creation of basic capability, increase in business value, creation of strategic options, and improved portfolio efficiency. Consider this: if a consultant makes a 10 percent improvement in a $1 million operation, it is worth $100,000. What this means is that you should not put high-cost consulting on low-dollar projects because there is very little ROC. But if the same consultant can make a 10 percent improvement on a $10 million project or a $1 billion business model, the ROC is much easier to identify as being in range. Identify the basis of the ROC and make it explicit.

Protect Your Investment

No consultant shows up ready to fail. Nor is she interested in running a business model that does not work for her, and the last thing she wants is a lost referral. Don't take advantage of the consultant by jerking around the schedule and missing commitments. Every cancellation represents lost income that cannot be made up. All consultants plan for gaps in their schedules, but at some point the rate becomes astronomical. If you engage a consultant, treat commitments to her with respect because in the end, it is your money and business model on the line.

Summary

There are times when getting support from outside the organization is critical to success. Consultants can hold up a mirror to the organization and provide the help the organization needs to bridge a gap in its competency or capacity. But the misuse of consulting talent and the overdependence on it are problematic. At some point, the organization must take a step up in capability to be able to bridge the gap on its own. Ultimately this means that a higher-level gap will open up, and perhaps that is another opportunity to engage outside help. The problem we have seen is that there is significant waste in the system of engaging consultants. Companies hire outside help with little definition of what the help will deliver and how value will be created. In some cases, we have seen consultants engaged for the purposes of providing a backdoor excuse, as in "Don't blame the executive team; after all, they engaged the highest-rated consulting company, and they only did what the consultants told them to do."

The common model for consultants and the common model for companies leave too much room for waste in the system. To reduce or eliminate such waste, you must first of all take ownership to understand your own business model so that you know what defines the transformation you seek. You need to move past problem solving when engaging transformation, so consultant engagements must be designed accordingly. You must understand where your organization stands on the "ready, willing, and able" aspects of change and seek support accordingly. Because every organization is unique, you must be suspicious of anyone offering a canned solution. Striking a balance between working in, working on, and working to transform is critical. Once you comprehend the benefit you are seeking and its implications for the business model, you can effectively select the help you need, the support required to make that person successful, and what it will take to keep your ROC high.

Ten Key Questions

1. Are you stuck in the typical consulting model?

2. Are you engaged in a typical company model with regard to consultants?

3. Do you know what part of the business model you are changing and why?

4. Have you successfully screened out consulting that takes the form of canned solutions?

5. Have you decided whether you want to add capability, add capacity, or simply get a specific thing done?

6. Is the consulting that you seek about readiness, willingness, or ability? How do you know?

7. Have you created a firm understanding of what you want from the consulting help you have?

8. How will the capability of the organization be influenced by the consulting you are engaging?

9. Have you created the support system inside the organization to make your consultant successful?

10. Do you know what the ROC is going to be?

CONCLUSION

Next Steps in Creating Better Models and Methods to Transform Organizations

Life is hard.

—M. *Scott Peck*

Everything should be made as simple as possible but not simpler.

—*Albert Einstein*

Difficulty and complexity are two things human beings tend to avoid. For the most part, people seem to be much happier with concepts that are easy on the brain, take little time to implement, and have the promise of immediate return on investment. This tendency gives rise to quick fixes that are simple and low cost. The problem with most of these approaches applied to transformation is that transformation does not come with speed or simplicity. We wish it did! It would make it so much easier to write this book and provide services to organizations making transformational changes. Unfortunately, it just doesn't work out that way.

Much has been written about our society's fascination with fast food, fast service, fast business results. We expect practically everything to be available at a drive-up window. The expectation of ease is nurtured by claims of fast-acting products promising miracle cures for everything from baldness to gastrointestinal distress. The pattern extends to consultants' claims of dramatic improvements with just a few simple changes. Nothing ends a sales conversation faster than the transaction's exceeding the complexity tolerance or the time expectations of the executive making the buying decision. The old adage about the confused mind always saying no would suggest that a street-smart salesperson should keep his presentation at an easily comprehended level even if it means oversimplification and an impossible timeline. Historically, business schools and consultants have attempted to reduce the complexity of situations by using the two-by-two matrix that converts business problems into four quadrants. The limitation with this approach is that there are more than two variables in play at all times in organizational transformation, and the gradation of the variables is not binary.

M. Scott Peck makes the point that as soon as we give up on the expectation that life should be easy, life actually gets easier. Einstein's point about theories being as simple as possible and no simpler suggests that we avoid dumbing down our approach to issues that are at a level of complexity above the two-by-two matrix. (Perhaps the irony has occurred to you that for someone to use a two-by-two box to illustrate the need to think outside the box defies basic rational thought.)

Our goal is to provide a path toward transformation by using concepts that are as simple as possible and no simpler, while also recognizing that what we're proposing may seem difficult. However, once you embrace the difficulty, things will become easier. We hope you will agree.

Beyond the Story Line

In the case of APC, we saw a company transform from a maker of discrete products to a provider of system solutions. Perhaps you are familiar with how DeBeers transformed its strategy from supply management to demand creation or how Nokia started as a company based on commodity manufacturing and transformed to a company centered on differentiated new technology. What is very difficult to see in looking at these three companies—or any other transformed enterprises—is what aspects of the business changed in order to transform the company.

In order to bring some visibility to how transformation can be orchestrated, we've created a model that attempts to link the parts and layers of an organization. It's not a matter of following lines and boxes in a process diagram. There is no formula or linear sequential path to transformation. In our experience, transformation is about orchestrating multiple elements, like a symphony with a few aspects of jazz. To accomplish transformation, one must work at seven "C" levels of the organization:

1. Core: the center of organization definition
2. Culture: the lens through which things get interpreted and accomplished
3. Context: the framing of the organization
4. Capability: the fundamental mechanisms for making things happen
5. Capacity: the level of demand that can be satisfied
6. Competency: the level and type of organizational expertise
7. Customer: the focus on outcomes for customers rather than on outputs

When a significant shift in customer outcome occurs, whether it is by way of a sweeping change in the market demand or in the market structure, or of desire on the part of the organization itself, it will touch off the need for transformation. When APC refocused on the need for power system solutions instead of power system products, the changes to the organization rippled through the layers of the organization, working back from the customer layer toward the core:

Customer outcome: from delivered product to turnkey solution

Competency: from product design to solution architecture

Capacity: from product manufacturing to system delivery

Capability: from manufacturing process to project management

Context: from product cost to system total cost of ownership

Culture: from control to collaboration

Core: from product maker to system provider

This is a greatly simplified outline of how a change in focus at the customer outcome layer implies changes all the way to the core of the organization. When leaders declare that they are going to modify the outcome target for the business, they are really saying that everything including the company brand is now in play. And with the company's brand in play, the link between people's identity and the organization is now also at play. In other words, transformation puts the elements of the company at all seven levels into flux.

By looking more closely at the levels of the organization, you can begin to see the many aspects that must be orchestrated in transformation.

Core

The core of the organization consists of purpose, identity, and long-range intention. (In *Executing Your Strategy*, this is referred to as *ideation*.) In transformation, the purpose—the reason that the company exists—can factor into the overall flux because the targeted customer outcome may not fit well with the existing purpose. As mentioned in Chapter Nine, Nikos Mourkogiannis speaks of four types of organizational purpose: heroism, altruism, discovery, and excellence. If a company is founded on discovery and the transformation demands excellence, some gene splicing of the basic organizational DNA will be required in order to get transformation to happen. If a merger is under way and the merged enterprises are of relatively equal size with a large disparity between organizational purposes, you can count on difficulties at the organization's core.

The second element of core is identity. Identity manifests itself as the internal and external brand along with all the interpretations of meaning of the brand. When a change to the business model causes flux to the identity of the company, it is no small consideration. More gene slicing.

The third and last element of core is long-range intention. Long-range thinking is not much of a draw these days. Of all the elements of the core of organizations, this one is typically the most rotten. The sustainability movement has somewhat brought this idea back into vogue, but for the most part, this is a lip-service element in most companies. Because there is no way to be out of alignment with something that does not exist, this area may present only a low transformation risk for most companies. It is also a potential opportunity to engage the human spirit in transformation by appealing to the idea of leaving a positive legacy for generations to come.

Context

Context is the layer of the organization that surrounds the organization core. In the context layer, people create goals, measurements, systems, organizational structure, technology, and strategy.

Goals are formal and informal expressions of what is to be achieved in the company. In the best case, these are specified and aligned vertically throughout the company. In the worst case, they are unexpressed vague notions. In transforming organizations, it becomes critical that goals be carefully designed to realign the organization to a new set of targets based on the changing nature of the customer outcome.

Measurements follow from goals. Measurement is critical in transformation because often the old metrics will not drive the right behaviors in the company. Some organizations struggle immensely to get an organization to change while attempting to maintain the same metric set.

Technology deals with the fundamental technological basis for the business model. Virtually every company depends on a type of information technology. (We would like to emphasize that the most important word in "information technology" is *information*.) In transformation, if the technology needs to change, then this becomes an element to add to the orchestration.

Systems are the ways information and work move throughout the organization, including the processes by which work is accomplished. Systems exist on two levels. On one level are the hard-coded systems that are embedded in computers, documented work flows, and procedures. On the second level are the soft-coded systems that are largely tacit knowledge embedded in specific people. Soft-coded systems present the greatest problem to transformation because substantive change can result in changes to staff. If a transformation includes a change from a system that deals with discrete parts to one that processes assemblies of parts into subsystems, and if the knowledge of how to modify the system is embedded in a particular person's head but that individual is not enrolled in the change effort, transformation might fail.

Structure is the element of context that is largely a tool to be used. There is no direct marketability of organizational structure. Adopting one structure or another is largely a matter of optimizing the ability of the organization to deliver goods and services to the customer. Leaders often know when they have the wrong structure, but the structure they have is the best they know of until they find a better one. Structure can be used to shape culture, goals, metrics, and strategy. In transformation, this is the simplest of the elements to orchestrate.

Transformation is likely to be defined as a shift of strategy. Strategy is the selection of the fundamental path to reach goals; it breaks down into market strategy, product or service strategy, and organization development strategy at a minimum. Transformation strategy deals with the required changes to the organization along with the transformation of the product or service being brought to market.

Capability

There are four critical capability areas to be considered in transformation. The first is portfolio management. Portfolio management is the capability of the organization to translate goals, metrics, structure, and strategy into a set of project and program investments. The portfolio manages the resources available to do the temporary work of projects and programs while providing for resources to operate the existing processes, including keeping the processes up-to-date. This is the most critical of the capabilities. Without effective prioritization based on transformational goals and resource allocation, transformation is largely a daydream with the potential to turn into a nightmare.

Program management is the capability of the organization to handle multiple projects that are interdependent in nature. Many of the things that have to do with transforming an organization require the integration of multiple pieces of work. The capability of an organization to segment large efforts into project pieces and then coordinate the pieces is critical to transformation. As with most layers of capability, competency, and capacity, program management also relates to portfolio management. If the organization has no capability in program management, it must make an investment in the capability, which means absorbing resources that could be deployed elsewhere. In addition, portfolio management relies on resource demand estimates from program management, so if the organization is low on program management skill, the capability of portfolio management is also diminished.

Project management is fundamental to program and portfolio management. If an organization lacks the capability to manage projects, the portfolio system does not receive accurate information, projects are not prioritized properly, execution is poor, and transformation will stall. Every project is a packet of strategy and transformation. Transformation depends on project success, not the other way around.

To understand process management, think of a business model as a recipe that is carried out through a process. What happens when the recipe (business model) needs to change, as it does in transformation? You get out the cookbook, alter the recipe, buy new ingredients, and start the next batch. What happens when the recipe is not written down? Oops. You need a new recipe, the old one is not written down, your ability to write recipes is somewhat limited, and therefore your ability to change a recipe nobody fully understood in the first place is limited. This is why process management is critical to transformation. Processes spell out the ingredients you need, and describe the steps required to make something from them. If process management is already a high-maturity aspect of the business, it is an asset. If not, it represents another required investment.

Competency

As we noted in Chapter Twelve, among various fields of expertise, Malcolm Gladwell found a commonality in the amount of experience at which a person becomes truly proficient. The point seems to be about ten thousand hours, which can be accumulated over five to ten years. When Captain Chesley B. Sullenberger III set the US Airways Airbus A320 down in the Hudson River on January 15, 2009, he had more than ten thousand hours flying time. In his postcrash interviews, he repeatedly said that he was "just doing what [he] was trained to do."

For people to have credibility and predictability, they must have at least ten thousand hours of relevant experience. The transformation challenge is to make sure we know where the "10k" experts need to be placed in the organization, what specific expertise they need to have, who they are, and where they are going to come from. When transformation involves changing things with which nobody has directly applicable 10k hours of experience, the transformation risk becomes much higher. Customers can see the competency level of a company almost directly. A company's brand can get damaged in short order when the competency of the company gets called into question. Transformation brings on this risk.

Capacity

Does your business model scale? If you can get all the other elements of the organization lined up, can you get the right amounts of the right ingredients to make a big enough batch to satisfy the demand and meet the business projections?

The two elements of transformation closest to the customer are competency and capacity. Both have the potential to make you or break you. You may have manufacturing capacity without distribution capacity, sales capacity without delivery capacity, delivery capacity without service capacity. It does you little good to attempt transformation unless you develop the capacity to go with the change in business models.

Culture

For the purposes of our discussion, we define culture as how things get done in organizations. People routinely blame their organization's culture for their inability to perform. Although this is convenient, it doesn't do much good. Culture cannot be seen directly, but only as a reflection of observing how people do what they do. Culture is evidenced by ways of doing work, language, dress, and communication styles, as well as by many other artifacts, some of which are very subtle. One way to look at culture is by observing an organization's artifacts, which in turn represent identity, long-range intention, and purpose. The artifacts take the form of acceptable behavior and expressions of "who we are," "where we are going," "why we do what we do," and so on. Brand images, brand interpretation, community relationships, expressions of what creates meaning, statements of what the organization is dedicated to, and communication about the future are all part of culture as it relates to core.

There is also a second level of culture that relates to context. Culture as a function of context is expressed in the way goals are set, measurements are selected, technology is deployed, systems are designed, and the organization is structured. Transformation may include modification of goals from a focus on product volume to a focus on project deliveries. Metrics may change from product cost to share of customer wallet. Technology may change from strictly in-house-produced items to third-party purchases. Systems designed to handle product-based transactions may need to create reports on the basis of project costing. These are all cultural changes. Every time an organization changes the way something is done, the product of a workflow, a means of measuring, or the criteria for success or promotion, it is altering culture. Culture shows up in capabilities, competencies, and capacities as the artifacts of how and what the organization is capable of, what it is good at, and how much it can deliver of what it does. Every modification to context, capability, competence, and capacity modifies culture at least slightly.

Customer

The point of transformation is to change the organization to serve the outcomes of an existing customer in a new way or deliver value to a new customer type. In working with organizations, we have found that the focus of many transformations are about changing technology, markets, channels, and so on, where the change in customer outcome is not well understood. We have seen transformations languish for lack of clarity in the area of understanding what specific outcome the organization is attempting to deliver to the customer. We don't think that transformation is likely without an understanding of customer outcome—unless an organization wants to rely on dumb luck.

A Transformation Model

When the elements of an organization that are the subject of transformation are grouped and arranged, the result might look something like the diagram in the following figure. One of the things we have noted over the years is how many people refer to transformation as an extraordinarily difficult undertaking. We agree. Small wonder. If we look at the overall task of what is to be orchestrated in terms of getting all the elements of transformation to work, it requires a lot of brain capacity. You can look at the model as a coin with two sides. On one side, the core is surrounded by context, capability, and so on. On the other side, you see that core is surrounded by culture, which extends all the way out to the interface with the customer. What we are suggesting is that culture has its foundation in the core of the enterprise and is the underpinning of context, competency, and capacity. We are also suggesting that this is why culture change is so often viewed as critical: everything a company does is guided by culture. The irony is that we don't change culture directly; we change it by changing context, capability, competency, and capacity. Culture is changed by modifying the artifacts of how things get done in the organization. This is probably a little hard to grasp, so here is what we suggest as an approach.

Organizational Transformation Framework

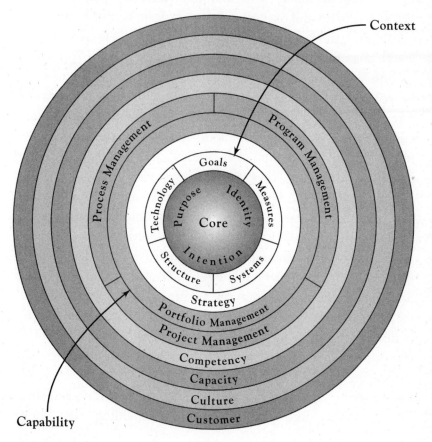

Develop Strategy Starting with Customer Outcome

The customer layer of the organizational transformation framework (OTF) is dedicated to the aspect of designing strategy on the basis of customer outcome. The key to transformation is to understand in very clear terms what customer outcome your organization is optimizing. This means knowing what the customer outcome is now and how it will change under transformation.

As an example, let's take another look at ALLDATA. ALLDATA produces a database of repair information that is critical in generating repair orders for automobiles. When a customer brings a car into a repair shop, the repair person can go to ALLDATA applications and find the information on how the repair must be made. This enables the repair person to give better estimates and execute the repair in the best fashion. When considering the customer outcome in this case, it is critical to ask which customer we are talking about. The car owner? The service technician? The shop owner? Each has a different outcome to be optimized. The car owner outcome will be associated with a repair she can trust. The technician outcome is the ease and completeness with which he does the job. For the shop owner, it is likely to be quality, consistency, and professionalism. In ALLDATA's history, these are all served very well.

Now consider the implications of implementing a new product line that focuses on the management of the shop itself. ALLDATA now must focus on a different outcome. The customer landscape is very different. The customer for shop management software is the shop owner. The repair technician and car owner are key to the process, but the central customer outcome has shifted from being associated with repair optimization to shop performance optimization. Because every shop is a little different in its cost structure, target market, basic competencies, and so on, the product and service delivery system must be modified to improve the overall performance of the individual shop. This is akin to shifting a company from providing a law library subscription service to providing a law practice software system. It is no small leap of logic to assume that a company that creates databases can provide business software. Strategy in this event must be considered from the outside in and then executed from the inside out. In ALLDATA's case, the change penetrates to the core due to the fundamental difference between a company that does repair action optimization and a company that does shop performance optimization.

Transform Starting with Core

When you have identified the strategy of choice and identified the customer landscape, you must look at the implications starting from the core of the organization working out. As we have discussed, the three fundamental aspects at the core are purpose, identity, and long-range intention. The transformation in the case of ALLDATA comes down to fundamental questions relative to purpose, such as the following:

- Is the change in the company more about discovering something, creating widespread benefit to people, saving the day on an issue, or doing a defined thing in a superior fashion?
- In the longer term, does the organization want to end up a professional services firm, a software tool company, or something else?
- In terms of identity, who are we as an organization? Are we more about being a library service or business model expert?

ALLDATA must answer these questions in relation to the targeted customer outcome. Once these questions are answered, the rest of the OTF can be put in place. For example, transforming to a business model expert will require a shift of culture from control to collaboration. It will require a shift of goals from subscriptions to account management. Metrics will have to shift from share of market to share of wallet. Structure will have to change from silos to matrix. Systems will have to be created that deal with product design, development, and deployment. Technology for client contact, monitoring, and support will be required. New marketing and sales systems must be added. Strategy must be modified to help differentiate the company in this space. Portfolio management must sort the priorities between keeping the legacy model healthy and building the new model. Project and program management must deliver the goods on time and within cost parameters. Fundamental investments in capacity and competency must be made in order to realign the company from the inside out. Knowing how to run the legacy business model and knowing how to run the new one are challenge enough, but add to that the competency requirement of leading the change between the two, and it is easy to see why transformation becomes such a major leadership issue.

How the OTF Relates to the Lessons

It is probably obvious why we created the OTF. It is an attempt to explain the arrangement of multiple aspects of an organization and help create a better way for leaders to conceptualize the organization while they examine what to do about transforming it. The framework is the result of our work with many organizations. After contemplating the lessons and attempting to find a pattern among the things leaders must deal with in order to apply those lessons, we developed this diagram as a means of describing and discussing the issues of transformation. Let's go through the lessons and relate them to the framework.

What Got You Here May Kill You There

If the core, culture, and context that build capability, capacity, and competence in your organization are well established, fundamentally departing from them becomes a significant legacy issue. When the core is no longer relevant to the strategy moving forward, there is a real dilemma. Should you keep going with a core that is obsolete, or do you make the tough choices to realign the business to the emerging environment? It has been said that if you dislike change, you may really hate irrelevance. But that is the inevitable choice. Survival does not go to the strong; it goes to the most adaptable.

Yesterday's Leadership Skills May Prevent Tomorrow's Success

Every ongoing organization has DNA based on its OTF. If the organization's business model ever worked, the DNA at least had validity at that point. The leadership challenge with transformation lies in making the dramatic shift in ability required to lead the transformed OTF versus the legacy OTF—including exercising the leadership skill to change leadership skills. Many leaders do not have the breadth of character to do so. An argument is that John Akers could not have pulled off the change that Lou Gerstner did under any circumstances. Carly Fiorina simply did not have the breadth to do what needed to be done with HP, especially amid a somewhat toxic combination of HP and Compaq recipes. This is a dilemma for transformation because the person calling for transformation may in fact be the reason for the lack of transformation.

There Is No Strategy If Nobody Knows What to Do

Strategy has been given too high a place in the hierarchy of discussion in business. There is more hype around strategy than there is substance. In a recent presentation, a consultant from a well-known consultancy said before a national audience that he did not have an agreed-on definition of strategy that would hold up in the room full of strategic planners. One of the leaders of a national organization on strategic planning said he does not even think strategic planning is a profession. All this leads us to say that unless you treat strategy in relation to the overall movement from core to customer outcome and realize that strategy is a critical piece of context but not the end game, you are unlikely to improve the dismal performance in strategic execution.

Transforming Strategy Requires More Than Expensive Software

Having the courage and insight to go a different way than the mainstream is a powerful form of leadership. Many of the banks that ended up tanking in the subprime mortgage crisis followed the conventional wisdom of assuming there would be a never-ending upward appreciation of real estate and increasing supply of people coming into the market for homes. So much for that line of reasoning. Only by understanding the OTF of your organization and translating them into a solid portfolio of investments are you going to be able to strike the best balance between who you are and what your customer desires as an outcome. No buyer of a subprime mortgage wanted a foreclosure of his or her property. But that is what the system was ultimately designed to do for buyers by focusing on loan origination volume and not on loan sustainability. Software can help, but the true opportunity lives in the rationale behind the calculations.

Transform Human Resources into a Strategic Advantage

We have reached the age of the human network. We went screaming past the industrial age, the information age, and the Internet age. It is now down to what we can get an organization to do through the way the organization is networked internally and externally. Unfortunately, at a time when HR organizations are most needed as a strategic partner, they are typically unprepared to answer the challenge. Many HR teams want a seat at the executive decision table, but are far short of having the credibility to engage the discussion. HR organizations must either step up to the challenge of designing organizations to be strong and adaptable across the OTF or accept an administrative role.

Your Customers Are Always Right, Except When They Aren't

By definition, the customer's desired outcome is always right, but there may be a difference of opinion as to how best to achieve the outcome. You can engage in satisfying the outcome or choose not to. The question is, does your organization have the means to satisfy the outcome? This would include the capability, capacity, and competence to do so. If you have a better means of satisfying the outcome than what the customer is asking for, then you have an opportunity to go for a win-win even though it is not exactly as prescribed by the customer. If the outcome is not in keeping with what your organization is about at its core, you would be better off staying out of the game unless you are willing to transform from the inside out for the sake of meeting the outcome. For example, buggy whips, kerosene lanterns, and floppy disks all became obsolete, but flexible rods for fishing poles, new portable lights, and new storage media continue to this day. These are examples of the essence of reinventing the business.

Don't Let Analysts Run Your Business

If you understand your business from core to customer outcome, the analysts are going to be the last of your worries, the reasons being that it is much harder to second-guess a business model that is well understood and much more likely that a well-understood business model will perform predictably. As a former executive of a Fortune 500 company recently pointed out, there is little value in spending two weeks getting ready to present quarterly numbers, two hours presenting them, and two weeks arguing with analysts as to why the numbers did not fit the analysts' models. We argue that paying attention to the OTF is a much better use of time, is more likely to create good business results, and is therefore of much higher value. Arguing with analysts will not improve your business. Better alignment and transformation have a chance. Invest accordingly.

Merger Is Not a Four-Letter Word

Or, at least, mergers don't have to stimulate the use of as many four-letter words as they have in the past. There are ways of assessing beforehand on an OTF level what matching aspects there are between organizations in mergers and joint ventures. By mapping the organizations across multiple dimensions, you can predict with a decent degree of accuracy where the disconnects are going to be. Where there are disconnects, you can create structural options or other mini-strategies to deal with the issues proactively. But doing so is only possible if you get out of the habit of merging on the basis of supposed economic synergies. Given the way mergers are typically executed, *synergies* is a synonym for "places we can cut." You would do well to remember that in the final analysis, the search-for-synergy approach is a worse bet than putting it all on red on a roulette table. Organizations need to be much more thoughtful about how they orchestrate mergers and take into account the implications of the OTF.

Who Melted My Cheese?

Think of an organization as being made from a unique recipe consisting of the elements of the OTF. When two companies are merged, the largest single risk is that value will ultimately be destroyed in the process. Seven out of ten mergers seem to go this way. The problem is that when companies of different recipes are merged, the numbers may look great, but the combination of the recipes is toxic. Sodium and water do not mix well unless you intend an explosion. Companies like Daimler and Chrysler do not mix unless you intend an implosion. The work to integrate two different recipes must take into account each organization's core, culture, context, capabilities, capacities, competencies, and customer outcomes. The issue seems to be that mergers are designed more on the value of numbers than on the value of the combined business model, including the people. Culture, structure, identity, and so forth are hard to add and subtract and therefore don't fit well with the typical means of doing M&As. We suggest that there is a much better way to "do the deal" than the way it is typically approached.

Spin Is Overrated for Creating Value

Let's say that a company has little developed sense of its core; therefore, its culture is weak and its context is confused, and that translates into strained capability, overloaded capacity, competency that does not quite fill the bill, and large gaps in meeting customer outcomes. Under those conditions, spin is all that is available to try to cover up the rust in the business model. Conversely, if the organization is strong, there is little if any need for spin. Honesty and candor become simple, straightforward, and easy to use in communication. Spin is a weak substitute for having your act together. The level of spin in an organization may be a really good metric for how much covering up is going on relative to the health of the organization in terms of the OTF.

Consultants Are Not an Excuse for Not Knowing Your Business

One of the problems that we have seen over the years is compartmentalization by consultants. Some will try to convince a company that success is a function of scorecards; others will attempt to create a panacea out of culture initiatives; others are strategists; still others are project management wonks. The problem starts with specializing in some area of the OTF and then trying to convince the customer that this one area is the pivot point for improvement. We say that the organization needs to understand how its OTF function and then find a consultant to deal with problems in relation to the overall understanding of the business. This will keep the consulting tail from wagging the organizational dog.

Lead Change Using a Road Map

The most perplexing question relative to the subject of transformation is often where to start. The subject seems so large and complex that it can be very daunting. Our experience tells us that there are a large number of ways to engage transformation. That said, there are easier ways and harder ways. The easier way to engage transformation is to have a road map that the executive team can hold in common as the organization goes about making transformational change a reality. In general, what must be recognized is that the end game of transformation is the same for everyone. No matter what organization you work for and what type of enterprise you lead, there is one fundamental ground rule of organizational transformation.

If individual accountability does not change, there is no transformation.

Understanding this ground rule can help cut through complexity. At the end of the day, if individuals don't have the change ingrained in their decision patterns and performance accountability, transformation is just a large, fancy concept and an expensive one at that. The real issue is, how does one create individual accountability? If you sense that it is easier said than done, you are correct. Keep in mind that we are advocating only as much complexity as necessary but enough to be sufficient.

There are three levels of the organization to concern your-selves with in creating a model for transformation:

1. *The organization level.* This could be a whole corporation, a division, a business unit, or a function. This is the top level of the organization for purposes of the model we are building.

2. *The process level.* This is the level at which work is done in the organization. It includes all planning, building, services, support, and decision-making processes.

3. *The individual level.* Everything at this level pertains to indi-vidual people in the organization. This is critical because although you are transforming an organization, there is really no such thing as an organization, only individuals who form some sort of collective. Anything done to transform an entity is enacted by individuals, not organizations.

We have three areas to consider within these three levels:

1. *Goals.* Plain and simple. This area concerns itself with the subject of achieving targets. One of the most critical deci-sions an enterprise must concern itself with is conveyed by the expression *intended achievements*. Although goals are set by individuals, some goals are for individuals, some are for the processes of work, and some for the overall group we call the organization.

2. *Translation.* In the translation area, you are concerned with naming the design elements that tie goals to management. The intentional translation of goals into strategy, organiza-tional behavior, and structure is central to moving them into the final area, which is management.

3. *Management.* This column is concerned with follow-through. At the organization level, management results in the communication of goals by the leadership and leader accountability to follow through on the goals. At the process

level, it includes the development and deployment of the measurement systems for processes, including leading and lagging measurements. At the individual level, it is the creation of individual accountability through performance management.

The figure here illustrates how these three areas and the three levels of organization interact.

	Goals	Translation	Management
Organization	What We Will Achieve Together	Design of Our Path, Team, and Culture	Leader Accountability
Process	What Our Processes Must Achieve	Processes to Set Priority and Execute	Process Accountability
Individual	What We Must Achieve Individually	Skills, Tools, and Systems	Individual Accountability

The key to making progress with this model is the close examination of the organizational core prior to setting goals (the upper left corner of the model). The problem organizations encounter with balanced scorecards comes from skipping the step of translating core to goals to strategy. This has led to the criticism that balanced scorecard systems are all head and no heart—that is, there is lip service paid to what is referred to as mission and vision, but without any real in-depth treatment of the subject of purpose, identity, and long-range intention prior to launching in to tables and spreadsheets. The second major shortcoming in the balanced scorecard approach is the lack of a real project management connection through portfolio management. In the center box of our model, "Processes to set priority and execute" is the center of the execution equation. If you do not get the prioritization and execution processes designed, implemented, and improved over time, transformation is not an option. Transformation simply cannot happen without portfolio control and project investment management.

There is much more work to be done to understand better ways to engage transformation and fill in the gaps in today's practices for organizational transformation. The two models we've presented in this chapter are works in progress, part of our attempt to find better answers. To go further, businesses will have to start asking better questions. The same old questions and frameworks that have created the problems organizations face are not going to lead organizations out of those problems. Einstein said long ago that people cannot solve their problems by using the same level of thinking they used when they created those problems. With this book, we have made a start by documenting some lessons and building some models. We offer them in the hope that you can use them in their current form, modify them to be more useful, and build on them to create better results for your organization.

Acknowledgments

I am deeply grateful to my coauthors, who believed in the value of undertaking the task of writing this book and had the courage to carry it out while maintaining grueling work schedules. This book contains advice we offer having lived through severe challenges together, and I will always be grateful for having the opportunity. I also thank my wife, Karen, for her unending support and patience. To the team at Jossey-Bass, Kathe Sweeney, Dani Scoville, Mary Garrett, and Michele D. Jones, I owe a debt of gratitude for having the confidence and foresight to follow through with this book and provide the hours of support to create and edit the manuscript. The constant support, great attitude, and encouragement have been a delight. I extend a special thanks to Carl Spetzler, Robert Lauridsen, Gideon Kunda, Neil Smith, William Malek, Suzanne Dresser, Craig Elkins, the team at Insights, and Professor Ray Levitt for their support and encouragement. To the team at ALLDATA, especially George Cusack, Jeff Lagges, Steve Gill, Kevin Culmo, and Frank McMaye, I acknowledge their courage and persistence in pursuing transformation. Rodger Dowdell is one of the most intriguing people I have ever met; he provided me with numerous insights into organizational transformation, including his focus on how unintended consequences are central to the executive perspective.

—Mark Morgan

For the honor of being able to work alongside the very dedicated employees of APC, I thank Ray Ballard and Hilary Murphy-Fagan for giving me my first shot at a role. I am grateful to Neil Rasmussen, Rodger Dowdell, and Dave Vieau for helping stretch my thinking in the simplification and solving of complex business problems. To Kate Beatty of the Center of Creative Leadership, I am grateful for the hours of support and encouragement through the years. It has been a privilege to have worked with Rob Johnson, Mark Morgan, and Dave Johnson on this project. For the passion and intellectual challenges we experienced while preparing this work, thank you.

For instilling in me a strong work ethic, a caring for all people, and a belief that no mountain is too high to climb, I thank my parents, Hugh and Patricia Cole.

Finally, I thank my wife, Denise, for her constant love and support, and our four sons, Hugh, Aidan, Aaron, and Peter, for their understanding as Dad has worked across the globe.

—Andrew Cole

I thank the numerous brilliant, energetic, creative, and inspiring colleagues with whom I have had the opportunity to work at APC in the last two decades. In particular, I acknowledge Neil Rasmussen for his vision, passion, and ability to simplify the most complex concepts. I thank Rodger Dowdell for the many challenges he laid out, stretching us to new heights. I thank Chris Di Napoli for getting me started with APC in the first place. I thank my co-authors Andrew, Rob, and Mark for their friendship and passion in all we have been through together. I also thank my father, Richard Johnson, for showing me how to be good to people while being an effective leader. Finally, I thank my wife, Ann, and my children, Katie, Charlie, and Joe, for all their support.

—Dave Johnson

I thank my wife, Rhonda, and my five kids, Alex, Michael, Bradley, Sam, and Krista, for their sacrifices, support, and patience throughout my career. I thank my father and mother, Rollie and Lois Johnson, who have been my mentors and coaches. I acknowledge the support of my brothers and sister as well as my good friend Steve Held. I also thank Neil Rasmussen, Doug Rademacher, David Vieau, and Rodger Dowdell for believing in me and helping me throughout my career. Last but not least, thank you to my great friends and teammates Mark Morgan, Andrew Cole, and Dave Johnson. Together we have moved mountains!

—Rob Johnson

About the Authors

Mark I. Morgan is CEO of StratEx Advisors, Inc., a consultancy designed to support organizational transformation and strategic execution. Mark is a consultant, coach, and master facilitator who specializes in leadership development, strategic execution, and organizational transformation. He is the lead author of the best-selling book *Executing Your Strategy* (Harvard Business School Press, 2008). He is the former chief learning officer of IPSolutions, Inc., and practice director of Stanford Advanced Project Management. Mark is a frequent guest lecturer at Stanford University, international conferences, and corporate executive sessions. He develops and delivers custom solutions and consulting at the most senior level of some of the world's most respected companies. Mark's background in strategic execution and organizational transformation stems from thirty years of experience, including a thirteen-year career with IBM, seven years as leadership consultant, the execution of two business start-ups, and ten years as a consulting educator in the field of strategic execution. Mark has worked in such companies as Cisco, Boeing, IBM, American Power Conversion, and Hewlett-Packard, and has delivered value for individuals, teams, and executives at all levels.

Mark has an MBA from Golden Gate University and a BS in engineering technology from California Polytechnic State University. He is PMP® certified and a Stanford Certified Project Manager (SCPM).

Andrew B. Cole is currently senior vice president of A123 Systems in charge of human resources and organization development, reporting to the CEO.

Andrew was born and raised on a farm, and his time as the Seminis global HR lead for Monsanto allowed him to get back to his roots. Prior to going to Monsanto, Andrew was the senior vice president of human resources for CPAC, a $4 billion division of Schneider Electric. In this role, Andrew played an instrumental part in the integration planning and execution of the merger between Schneider Electric and American Power Conversion (APC). Prior to the merger with Schneider, Andrew held the position of global vice president of human resources and organization development with APC. In this role, Andrew was instrumental in the design of the organizational changes that were key in APC's transformation from a channel-focused organization to a solutions provision company. Irish by birth, Andrew has extensive global experience in dealing with business issues and the conversion of HR to a true business partner. Andrew holds a BA and an MS from Regis University, Denver, Colorado.

David R. Johnson is senior vice president at APC, a business unit of Schneider Electric. Dave leads a multibillion-dollar division of APC responsible for developing and marketing products for APC's small and medium business customers as well as consumers. Previously at APC, Dave also served as senior vice president of worldwide sales, leading a team of more than two thousand people. Since joining APC in 1989, he has held other senior positions in marketing, product development, and sales management. In late 1999, Dave left APC and participated in two start-up ventures before rejoining APC in 2003. He graduated with a BS in applied economics from Cornell University and began his business career with GE Plastics in corporate finance. Dave's diverse background in executive management, finance, sales, marketing, and product development gives him strong perspectives on a myriad of business and organizational issues. He lives with his wife and three children in Newport, Rhode Island.

Robert J. Johnson is currently responsible for A123 System's Energy Solutions Group. Rob has over twenty years of leadership and management expertise in power systems and control solutions. Rob has led small organizations of ten people and organizations of more than ten thousand. He has taken part in or led several acquisitions and integrations as well as participated in major company transformations.

Prior to joining A123 Systems, Rob served as senior vice president and president of North America at APC-MGE, a global provider of critical power and cooling services. Rob joined APC in February 1997, when APC acquired the software management company he cofounded, Systems Enhancement Corporation. Upon joining APC, Rob became general manager of this group and eventually served as president and chief executive officer of APC, prior to its acquisition by Schneider Electric for $6 billion, which combined its industry leadership with that of MGE UPS Systems.

Index

Page references followed by *t* indicate a table; followed by *fig* illustrated figure.